MAKING WOOD BANKS

Harvey E. Helm

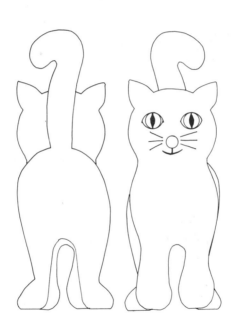

**Home
Craftsman
Series**

 Sterling Publishing Co., Inc.   New York

Distributed in the U.K. by Blandford Press

Edited and designed by Hannah Reich.
Hand lettering by Joan Columbus.

Library of Congress Cataloging in Publication Data

Helm, Harvey E.
  Making wood banks.

  (Home craftsman series)
  Includes index.
  1. Wooden coin banks.   2. Woodwork.   I. Title.
II. Series.
TT200.H35   1983   745.593   83-474
ISBN 0-8069-7714-0 (pbk.)

Copyright © 1983 by Sterling Publishing Co., Inc.
Two Park Avenue, New York, N.Y. 10016
Distributed in Australia by Oak Tree Press Co., Ltd.
P.O. Box K514 Haymarket, Sydney 2000, N.S.W.
Distributed in the United Kingdom by Blandford Press
Link House, West Street, Poole, Dorset BH15 1LL, England
Distributed in Canada by Oak Tree Press Ltd.
% Canadian Manda Group, P.O. Box 920, Station U
Toronto, Ontario, Canada M8Z 5P9
Manufactured in the United States of America
All rights reserved

CONTENTS

This book is dedicated to my lovely wife, Joan, and my five children who put up with a woodworking nut for a husband and father, to the town of Darien, Connecticut, for the opportunity to teach some of the greatest kids on earth, and finally to my students who keep me on my toes and without whose challenge for more, new, and different projects this book would not have been written.

INTRODUCTION

Welcome to the banking business—wooden, that is. The banks in this book were developed over a period of six years. They are the result of my students wanting to make something other than a footstool or bookshelf.

The first bank we made was the piggy bank in 1976. From then on the students would say, "You ought to make a whale bank," and in a day or two we would be making whales. Some of the designs came easily (the owl was designed and built on one of my lunch breaks). Others, like the rooster, took more than a year to develop. The point is, you can design your own bank using the same general ideas in this book. Ideas for designs can come from any source: newspapers, magazines, hobbies, professions, anything!

Finally, these banks are very simple to make, but please read the directions first. Also, just because my seventh graders can make them, do not think they are only for kids. I am sure that some will be a challenge for those of you who are experts.

I wish you much luck, success, and fun in the banking business.

Harvey E. Helm

METRIC CONVERSION CHART

Inches	Millimetres	Inches	Millimetres
$\frac{1}{32}$	8.0	1	25.4
$\frac{1}{16}$	1.6	2	50.8
$\frac{1}{8}$	3.2	3	76.2
$\frac{3}{16}$	4.8	4	101.6
$\frac{1}{4}$	6.4	5	127.0
$\frac{5}{16}$	7.9	6	152.4
$\frac{3}{8}$	9.5	7	177.8
$\frac{7}{16}$	11.1	8	203.2
$\frac{1}{2}$	12.7	9	228.6
$\frac{9}{16}$	14.3	10	254.0
$\frac{5}{8}$	15.9	11	279.4
$\frac{11}{16}$	17.5	12	304.8
$\frac{3}{4}$	19.1	18	457.2
$\frac{13}{16}$	20.6	24	609.6
$\frac{7}{8}$	22.2	36	914.4
$\frac{15}{16}$	23.8		

TOOLS

The construction of these banks is very simple, and few tools are required. I would advise you to buy the very best tools you can afford as they will give you longer use, generally will work better, and will be more economical in the end. With few exceptions it does not pay to buy cheap throwaway tools.

To get into the bank business you will need the following:

One coping saw and a package of blades. (You will break a few blades before you learn to use the saw correctly.)

One drill. I recommend a low cost ¼″ capacity electric drill. This will cost you about half what a hand drill (egg-beater type) costs, and the electric power is handy, but you can use a bit and brace or hand drill.

One hole-saw set. The nesting kind with seven sizes from ¾″ to 2½″ is okay, but a mandrel and individual saws are of much better quality.

Assorted twist drill and spade bits. These can be purchased as needed.

Files and rasps. One-half round cabinet file 8″ long plus a good file handle. (*Note:* The file handle is very important. A poor one will hurt your hand and fall off and be a real annoyance. Try the handle first and see if it is comfortable. There are two basic kinds: One screws onto the file tang [end], and the other is driven on. Stay away from the driven-on kind as it works loose and falls off.) You also need a one-half round cabinet rasp.

Vise. You will need a means of holding your work secure. If you have a workbench with a vise, great! If not, a small vise clamped to a table will do.

Clamps. If you are going to make your banks without using nails you will also need some clamps for holding the pieces together until the glue dries. These can be wide-opening, spring clamps (4¼″ wide) or *wooden hand screws* (more expensive, but better). You can make your own clamps of ¾″-thick plywood scrap by cutting C's and using wedges. Check with a local cabinetmaker or woodworking shop. Most of them throw out scrap that would make fine clamps. The size of the clamp is determined by the thickness of the parts to be clamped. When cutting out the "C," keep the wood at least 1½″ wide all around the "C" for strength. The opening of the jaws should be kept parallel. You will need at least four clamps of each size to get even pressure around the bank. You will also need some wedges to drive in between the "C" and the work. Cut the wedges from ¾″-thick wood and taper from 0″ to 1″ or more. A long, gradually tapered wedge will hold better than a short, steep one.

When used, the clamp is placed on the work and the wedge is tapped in between with a hammer. Sometimes two wedges are used together. Drive one wedge in from each side. (See illustration.)

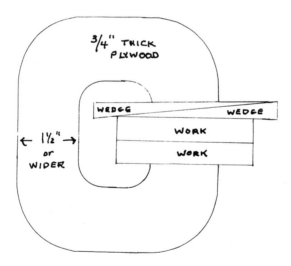

One *claw hammer,* 13 oz.
One *accurate ruler, tape measure, or folding rule.* Do not use a school ruler or a yardstick as these are not accurate.

You may have a whole shop full of tools, but these few simple tools will make any bank in this book.

MATERIALS AND SUPPLIES

All the banks in this book can be made from 1″ × 6″ lumber and ½″ × 6″ lumber. (Note: A 1″ × 6″ board will actually be ¾″ × 5½″, and a ½″ × 6″ board will be ½″ × 5½″.) I use pine mostly, as it is the least expensive and most available in my area, but any wood will do. Soft wood is easier to work with.

Visit a local cabinet shop or other woodworking business and inquire about their scrap or waste. If you stay out of their way and do not bother them, they will usually be glad to have you haul away scrap. The biggest piece of wood you need for these banks is ¾″ × 5½″ × 8½″. In some cases, you can use plywood. The stripes the plies make look very decorative, but be sure there are no voids (holes) in between the plies that could show up on the edges of the bank. This would spoil the appearance.

Glue. Any good glue for wood is okay, but "yellow" (alphatic) glue is the best. It has more grab and sets faster than white (casein) glue, which is a big advantage. Many times you can glue the parts together without clamping and resume working in as little as one hour's time.

Try this little experiment: Take two small pieces of wood, spread yellow glue on the surface of one (a thin coat will do), and place the second piece onto the glue. Slide them back and forth a few times to spread the glue. Set the pieces aside for five to ten minutes. You will have considerable difficulty getting them apart, if you can at all. Try the same test with white glue and you will see the advantage of yellow glue. Yellow glue can also be sanded, which is very important in this work.

Template-making equipment. You will need some paper, light (shirt) cardboard, and Number 2 pencils. Pencil marks are easier to remove from wood than are ball-point pen or other ink marks.

Sandpaper. Garnet or aluminum oxide are best. They cost more but last longer than flint. You will need 60, 80, 100, and 150 grit for sanding the wood and some finer wet or dry sandpaper for the finish later. Sandpaper sheets come 9″ × 11″ and can be cut to 3″ × 3½″ pieces, to get nine pieces from each sheet.

Small nails or brads. If you choose to nail the parts together, use nails 1½″ long, or shorter.

Paints, stains and wax. See page 15 for information on finishing the banks. Be extra sure to use non-toxic finishing materials since these banks will draw the attention of small children who love to put things in their mouths. Food color diluted in water makes excellent stain in a variety of colors. Wax in paste form is a good finish material. Mineral oil or vegetable oil is also good for the hand-rubbed look.

ENLARGING PATTERNS (USING THE SQUARES METHOD)

Any drawing or pattern can be made larger or smaller by superimposing a grid on the drawing and copying what you see in each square onto larger or smaller squares. The squares keep the drawing in proportion. With a little practice an

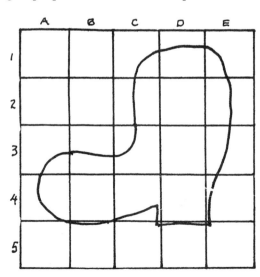

accurate drawing can be made with little effort. Begin by making a grid the size desired. If you copy the design from ¼″ squares onto ½″ squares you will get a design twice the size of the original. Number the squares on the side and letter them across the top. (See illustration.)

Start with one square and make marks where the lines cross from this square to the next. Continue until you have marked each place where lines cross on the larger grid. Now connect the lines in one smooth continuous line to give you the larger design. The pattern can now be transferred to cardboard, or directly to the wood, using carbon paper.

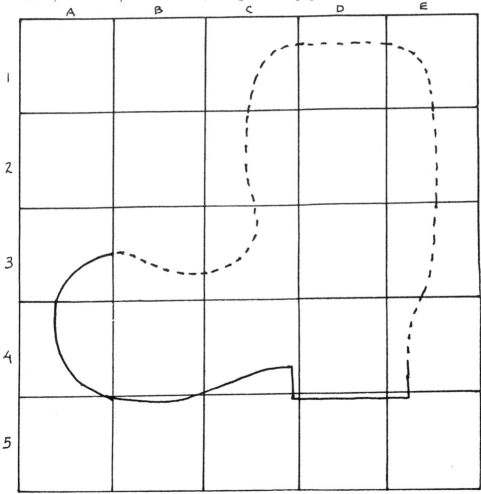

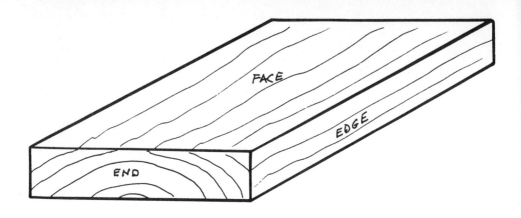

CONSTRUCTION TIPS

All the banks with the exception of the truck are constructed using the laminating process. This means the banks are built up by glueing the surface of the wood together. Pick up a rectangular piece of wood and look at the six surfaces it has. *The face* is the large flat surface, sometimes called the top or bottom. *The edge* is the narrow surface, running the length of the board on each side. The grain is fairly straight. *The end* is the section that shows the tree's growth rings.

These surfaces have different grain characteristics and grain is very important in working with wood. You may glue any of these together except the end grain. If you try to glue the end grain you will have a very weak joint. The banks are made by glueing the wood together face to face to get a block of laminated wood 3" thick, or as thick as the bank you are making requires. If the face of the wood is smooth and flat or straight, you can glue the parts together without clamps, using yellow glue. If the wood is warped or cupped, you will have to clamp the parts flat until the glue sets (about one hour for yellow glue and about four or more for white glue).

If you are going to make more than one bank—and you probably will, because everyone who sees one will say, "Oh, would you make me one?"— take the time to make cardboard templates for the parts. You can save much time if you have templates to trace around. You can change the size of the bank (larger or smaller) by using the grid method.

When you have the full-size pattern, the next step is to lay out each part

on the wood. This step must be carried out with care and planning. The grain must run in the direction on each piece that will give maximum strength. You should avoid knots or place the part so the knot is hidden. (See photo for layout of the rooster parts.) Sometimes a knot can be used as part of the design, i.e., an eye.

The grain should run the length of narrow parts that need to be strong, i.e., the rooster's legs. The parts in the photo were laid out using a soft-tipped marker for extra contrast. Use a Number 2 pencil, as it is easy to sand off or erase; ink soaks in and could spoil the looks of the finished bank.

Once the parts are laid out, cut them out to shape and size. If you are using a coping saw, cut each part out as close to the line as you can, but be sure to leave the line showing. If you cut the line off you will have no reference point when filing or sanding. (I have seen some funny-looking parts when students took the line off and kept on sanding, completely changing the shape of their projects.)

When you are sawing, keep the saw at a 90° angle from the surface to make a square edge. Saw with a smooth back-and-forth motion. Do not use very much pressure or you will break a lot of blades and get a very rough cut. Try to get a feel for how the saw wants to cut, and you will have smooth edges. Care in sawing saves a lot of filing and sanding time and effort later.

When the parts are cut out examine them and see if you need to correct any cuts. Sometimes it is easier to true up a cut before assembly. This is because later it will be in a hard-to-work position. The rooster is an example of this. The heart, turtle, and owl banks are all easier to smooth out after the body is glued up.

If you will be using a band saw it may be easier to glue up the pieces first and then cut out the shape. For example, the owl bank can be glued up first. The two center body pieces can be glued and then the middle cut out. Then glue the outer pieces to the center and cut the outside shape all at once.

When the parts are glued together you can start smoothing the edges and getting the shape of the bank. I find that the best way to do this is with a fine-tooth patternmaker's wood rasp, half-round, 8″ long, but you can also use a fine-tooth cabinet rasp. Take your time with the filing and shaping as this is often what gives character to the bank. A little more off in one place, a little less in another, and you can change the whole appearance of the bank.

After you have worked awhile, stand back and look at it or get someone else's opinion. The better the job you do with the rasp, the less filing you will have to do. When you have rounded all the corners and have the shape you want, start with the cabinetmaker's file. (Some people like the rough texture of the rasp and go right from there to sanding.) File the rasp marks smooth. You can do a really good job with the cabinet file and again it will save on the sanding. I usually start with 80-grit sandpaper after filing. If you have some rough spots you could not file, use 60-grit sandpaper to smooth them out. Next I use 100 grit and then 120 grit. This will usually be smooth enough for the finish. Remember, *sand only with the grain.* It will take about fifty strokes with the grain to remove the grossgrain scratches from one careless stroke across the grain.

Most of the banks require a 1½″-diameter hole drilled into the body for coin removal. This can best be done after the body is glued up, as it is easier to locate the hole then. Use a 1½″-diameter hole saw in the ¼″ electric drill to make this hole. The plug that is pressed into this hole is cut out a little bit oversized and is sanded on a slight taper (edge) for a tight fit. If you have a disc sander it will be very handy for this step. Sand at about a 4° angle.

The plug should only go about halfway into the hole without pressure. This will ensure a tight fit which will get looser with use. The plug is glued to the back of the part that will cover the hole. When dry the part is used to twist the plug into the hole. This makes it a secret. Everyone will ask, "How do you get the money out?" (See illustration of tapered plug glued to part.)

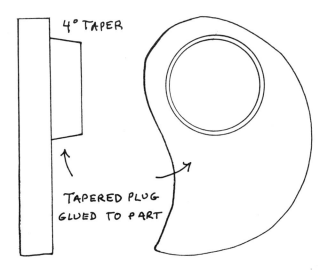

4° TAPER

TAPERED PLUG
GLUED TO PART

When you cut out the inside to hold the coins you can usually cut from the outside through the coin slot. If this is not possible, drill a ½" hole through the piece. Take the blade out of the coping saw, insert it through the hole and replace the blade into the saw frame. When you have finished the cut, reverse the process. The blade can be turned in the frame to reach difficult areas.

Most of the eyes are made with a ½" spade-type bit. Drill about ⅛" deep. This makes an eye with a pupil and is simple. You can also make eyes to glue on from dowels, chair buttons, etc.

FINISHING
I like a clear finish best for these banks as it shows off the natural beauty of the wood, but this is mostly personal choice. Sometimes different-colored woods are used to give contrast, such as mahogany with pine. A similar effect can be had with stain or paint. (Again, as mentioned in the chapter on materials, use non-toxic stains and/or paints.)

A very nice finish is hand-rubbed oil or wax. Simply apply and rub with a soft cloth to a nice lustre. If you use a clear finish such as lacquer or varnish, apply as directed on the container. Use three or four thin coats and sand lightly between each with fine sandpaper (200 grit or finer). Apply a coat of wax and polish with a soft cloth.

NAILING

If you choose to glue and nail your banks together, try to position the nails where they will not show. If a nail will show, "set it." (Punch it below the surface.) Using the point of another nail, insert a small amount of glue and sand over the hole immediately. The sawdust will mix into the glue and hide the hole, or at least make it less visible.

All the banks that are rectangular blocks with face-mounted parts use the same body, so you can make several bodies at one time and use them to create different banks. For example: The television, flower, dove, etc.

HEART

Begin construction of the heart by laying out the five parts on ¾"-thick stock. On the front- and back-face pieces the grain must run vertically, or top-to-bottom, so the points will not break when the base is inserted between them. The grain also runs the length of the base. Cut the parts to shape. Glue the two center parts together and when dry cut out the center, starting at the coin slot at the top. This is not something to be fussy about, as no one will see it. Keep the coin slot about ⅛" wide and straight, so the coins can enter but not fall out. Glue the front and back pieces to this hollow center piece. (Note: If you want a thinner bank you can use ½"-thick pieces for the front and back, but the center must be 1½" thick to take the coins.) When the glue has set, drill a 1½"-diameter hole for coin removal between the two points of the heart into the cavity.

Make the base piece slightly oversized, and sand to fit tightly between the two points covering the hole. Rasp, file, and sand until the edges are smooth and the corners nicely rounded. Apply the finish of your choice.

FRONT AND BACK

Make two pieces ½" thick

BASE

Make one piece ¾" thick

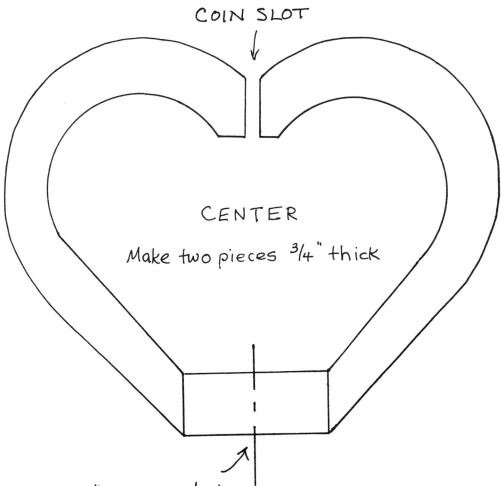

COIN SLOT

CENTER

Make two pieces $3/4$" thick

Drill $1\frac{1}{2}$" diameter hole
after parts are assembled.

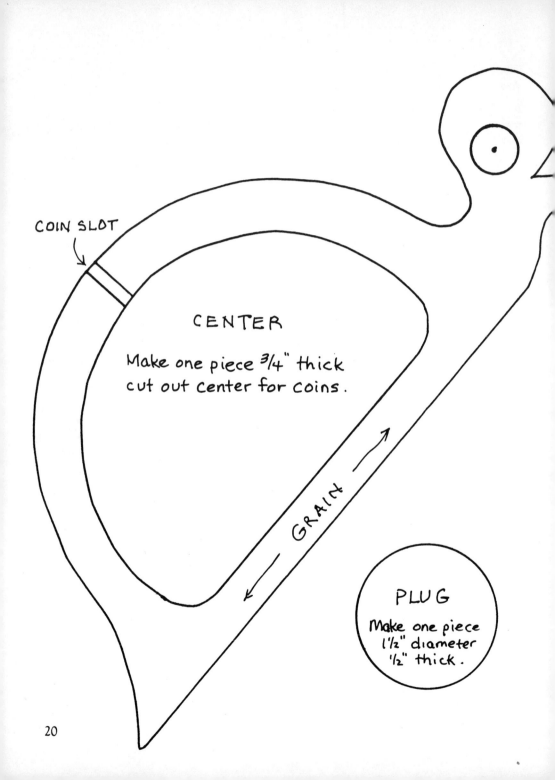

COIN SLOT

CENTER

Make one piece 3/4" thick
cut out center for coins.

GRAIN

PLUG

Make one piece
1½" diameter
½" thick.

20

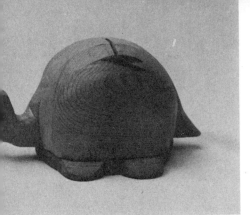

TURTLE

The turtle bank is an easy bank to make, only slightly more difficult than the heart bank. Transfer the patterns onto the wood. The grain in the center piece must run towards the head for strength in the neck and tail. Cut the center out of the three middle pieces (for the coins). Glue all five body pieces together. Be careful to align all the pieces, to minimize filing and sanding. Before filing, drill the 1½"-diameter hole in the center of the bottom of the turtle for coin removal.

Locate and drill ½"-diameter holes ⅛" deep for the eyes. Rasp and file the corners to make the body round. Fit the feet to the bottom of the turtle so the body blends into the bottom. Glue the plug to the center of the bottom. (See Construction Tips, page 12.) File and sand until smooth. Finish as desired.

FRONT VIEW,
showing lamination,
base, and head.

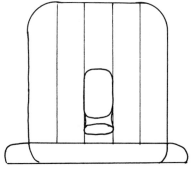

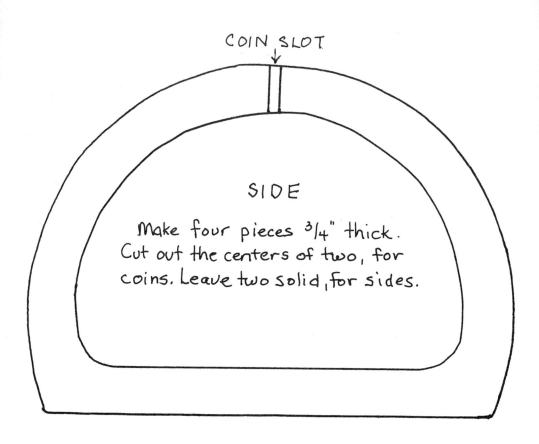

COIN SLOT

SIDE

Make four pieces $3/4$" thick.
Cut out the centers of two, for
coins. Leave two solid, for sides.

BOTTOM, showing feet

Make one piece ½" thick.
Cut and shape sides to fit bottom
of turtle. Glue plug to center.

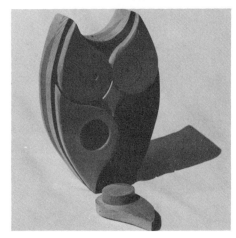

OWL

Begin making the bank by cutting two ¾"-thick pieces of wood to 5½" × 8½". These pieces will be the center of the owl. Draw the pattern onto the face of these two pieces and cut out the shape. Cut the outside as close to the line as possible without cutting the line off. The coin slots must line up and be straight to allow coins to drop, but alignment of the inside cavity is not critical. Next, cut two pieces of ½"-thick stock to 5½" × 8½". Draw the pattern on the face and cut the outside shape only. These pieces are the front and back of the owl. These four pieces are now glued and clamped to form the hollow body of the owl. Care in aligning the pieces while glueing will save much work later in filing and sanding.

While the glue is setting, cut out the surface-mounted parts—the two eyes, beak, side, and wing. Make the eyes by drilling with a 1½" hole saw about ⅛" deep. Next, drill the pupil with a ½" spade bit ⅛" deep. Then glue the eyes, beak, and side to the front of the owl body. If the faces of these parts are flat and you use yellow glue, there is no need to clamp them. When the glue has set, rasp, file, and sand until the owl is smooth. Drill a 1½"-diameter hole through the side piece into the body cavity. Be sure the hole will be covered by the wing. Glue the 1½"-diameter plug to the underside of the wing. Sand and finish as desired.

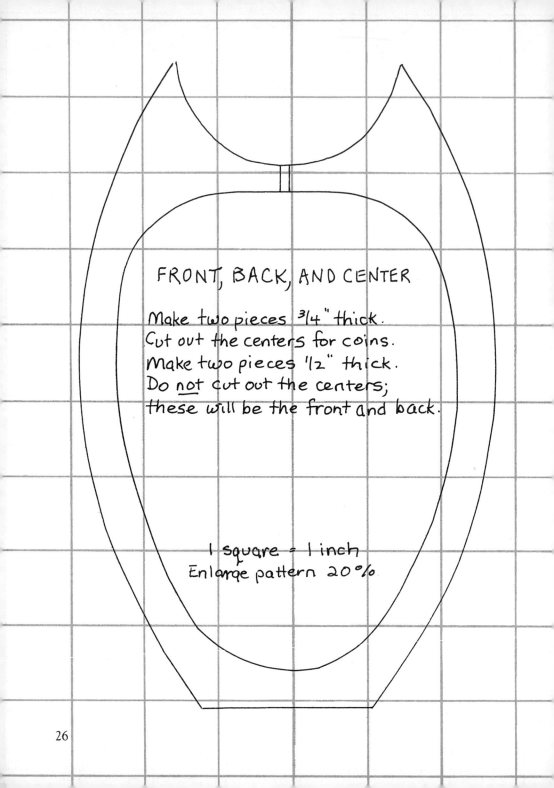

FRONT, BACK, AND CENTER

Make two pieces $3/4$" thick.
Cut out the centers for coins.
Make two pieces $1/2$" thick.
Do not cut out the centers;
these will be the front and back.

1 square = 1 inch
Enlarge pattern 20%

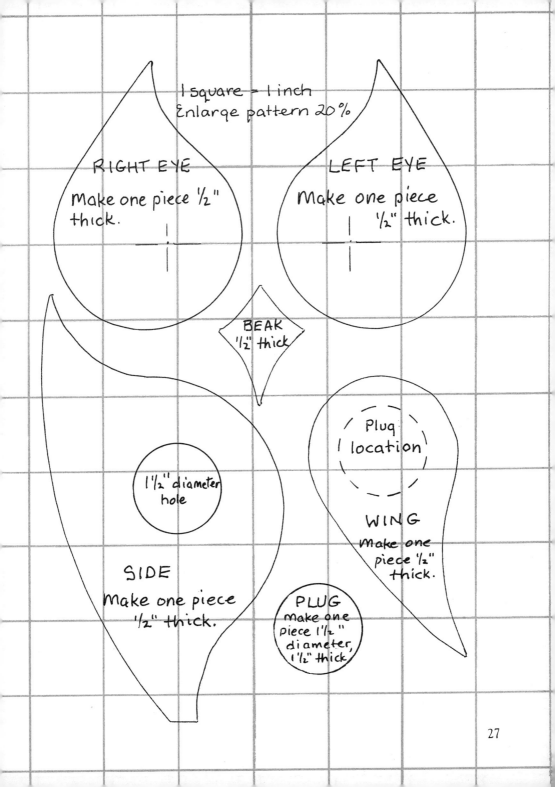

1 square = 1 inch
Enlarge pattern 20%

RIGHT EYE

Make one piece ½" thick.

LEFT EYE

Make one piece ½" thick.

BEAK ½" thick

Plug location

WING

Make one piece ½" thick.

1½" diameter hole

SIDE

Make one piece ½" thick.

PLUG

make one piece 1½" diameter, 1½" thick.

27

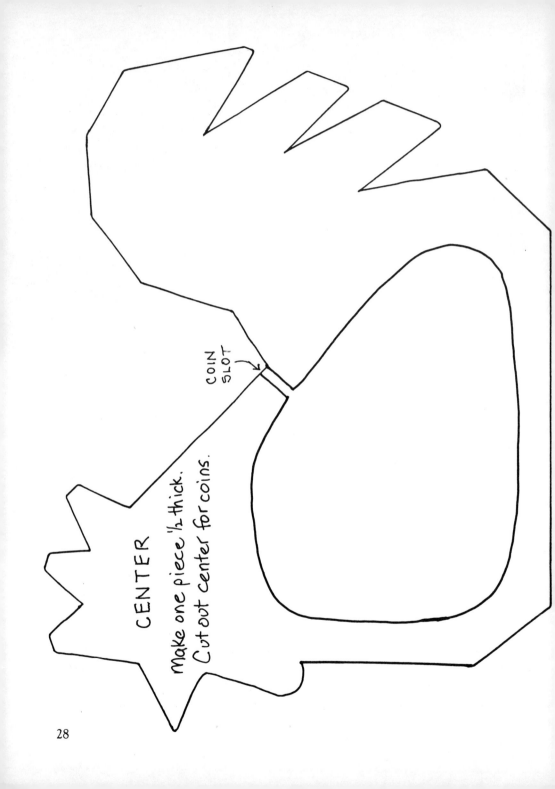

COIN SLOT

CENTER

Make one piece ½ thick.
Cut out center for coins.

ROOSTER

This is an easy bank to make. All the wood should be ½" thick. The center piece—the tail, comb, and beak—should be made from dark wood (mahogany or cherry). The rest can be light wood (pine or yellow poplar). Begin by transferring the patterns to the wood. The leg pieces require the grain vertical for strength. Cut out all the pieces, including the center of the three middle pieces. Sand all the edges before assembly. Glue and clamp the three middle pieces and when dry, cut the coin slot straight across these parts just above the tail. This will make a slot ⅛" wide by 1½" long.

Drill a ¼"-wide hole through the head for the eyes. Drive a ¼" by 2" dowel through this hole for the eyes, leaving ¼" on each side. Glue and clamp the sides to the body. Drill a 1½"-diameter hole on one side under the wing position. Glue the wing to the other side. Make a 1½"-diameter plug ½" thick. File or sand a 4° taper on the edge of the plug to make a tight fit in the body hole. Glue the plug to the back of the wing. Sand the entire bank to remove all saw marks, file marks, and pencil marks. Apply the finish.

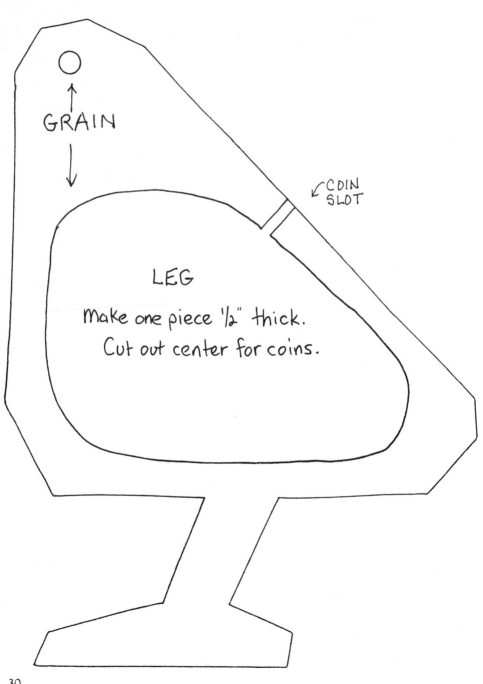

GRAIN

COIN
SLOT

LEG

Make one piece 1/2" thick.
Cut out center for coins.

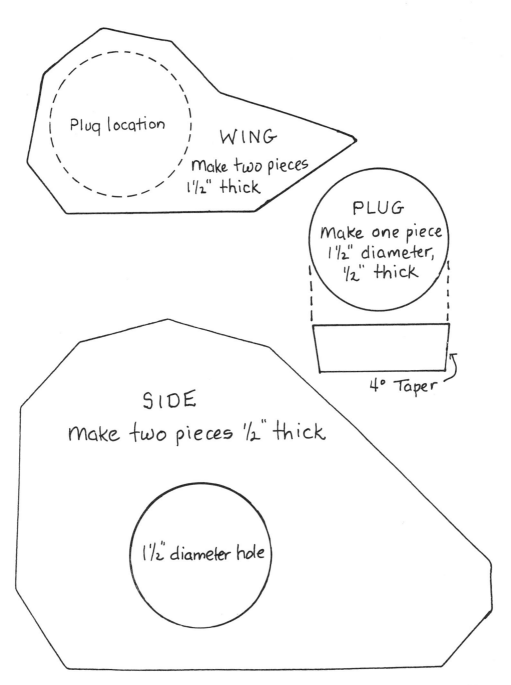

Plug location

WING
make two pieces
1½" thick

PLUG
Make one piece
1½" diameter,
½" thick

4° Taper

SIDE
make two pieces ½" thick

1½" diameter hole

These four pieces of wood (the two center sections are already glued together) form the basis for all the face-mounted banks in this book.

FLOWER

You will need four pieces of wood ¾″ × 5½″ × 8½″ for the body of this bank. Nail and glue two of these together for the center of the bank. Space fourpenny finish nails around the edges where they will not interfere with cutting out the center and will be covered by the front and back. Cut out the center for the coins, as shown in the drawing. Glue and clamp the front and back onto the center section.

The face parts should be cut out, sanded, and stained before glueing to the face of the bank. Use food coloring for stain. Make the flowers red or yellow, the leaves and stem green, and the flowerpot brown. The hole and plug for removing coins are behind the flower. The top corner of the round part of the flower should be rasped heavily to make it quite round.

(Note: For this and the subsequent rectangular banks, you can experiment with different shapes or give the banks square corners if you wish, to create other variations.)

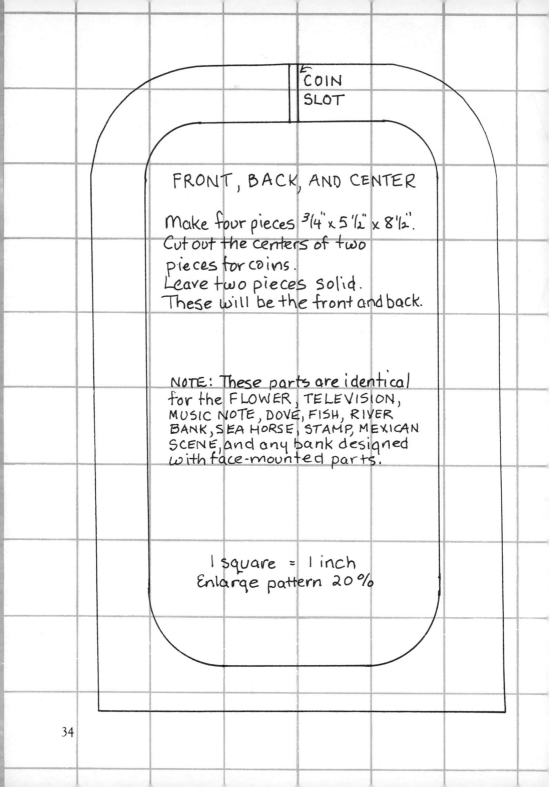

COIN
SLOT

FRONT, BACK, AND CENTER

Make four pieces ³/₄" x 5¹/₂" x 8¹/₂".
Cut out the centers of two
pieces for coins.
Leave two pieces solid.
These will be the front and back.

NOTE: These parts are identical
for the FLOWER, TELEVISION,
MUSIC NOTE, DOVE, FISH, RIVER
BANK, SEA HORSE, STAMP, MEXICAN
SCENE, and any bank designed
with face-mounted parts.

1 square = 1 inch
Enlarge pattern 20%

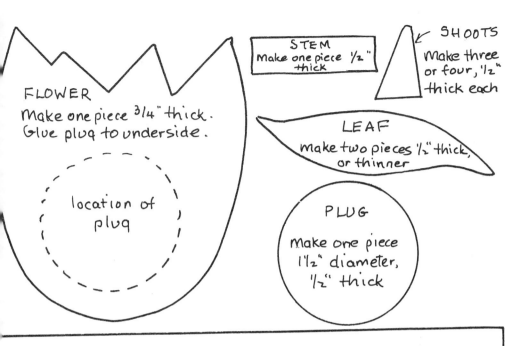

FLOWER
Make one piece ¾" thick.
Glue plug to underside.

location of plug

STEM
Make one piece ½" thick

SHOOTS
Make three or four, ½" thick each

LEAF
make two pieces ½" thick, or thinner

PLUG
Make one piece 1½" diameter, ½" thick

FLOWERPOT RIM
Make one piece ¾" × 1" × 5½"

FLOWERPOT BOTTOM
Make one piece ½" × 2" × 5"

SCREEN

Make one piece ½" thick

KNOB
make two pieces:
make one ½" thick;
make one ¾" thick (for plug).

TELEVISION

Lay the parts on the wood and cut them to shape. Glue the two center sections together (see page 34 for pattern), and cut a ⅛"-wide coin slot across the middle into the center. Glue the front and back onto the center pieces. Select a picture from a magazine and glue it in position on the T.V. screen. Glue the frame over the picture.

Drill a 1½"-diameter hole under one of the knobs into the cavity. The knobs have ½" × ½" strips glued across the top. The knob that will fit into the hole should be ¾" thick and tapered slightly to fit tightly into the hole. Glue the speaker and other knob to the front. Drill two ¼"-wide holes on an angle near the back on top of the set. Insert ¼"-wide dowels with small beads glued on top for antennae. Sand and finish as desired.

SPEAKER

Make one piece ½" thick

KNOB ATTACHMENT
make two pieces ½"
thick

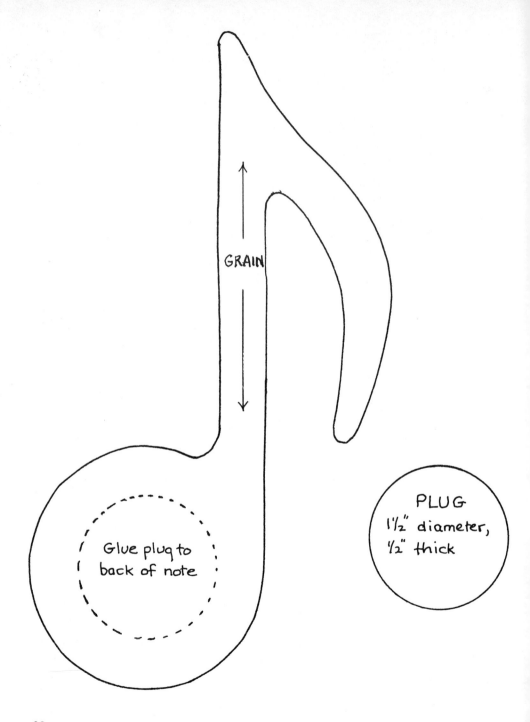

GRAIN

Glue plug to
back of note

PLUG
1½" diameter,
½" thick

MUSIC NOTE

Again this bank uses the same body as the flower, television, and other rectangular banks. Use the directions and center section pattern from the flower bank, and then cut out the note. (See illustration.) The note should be made of a strong hardwood or high-grade plywood for strength. File and sand the edges round and paint the note black. The front or background should be a light color for contrast. Drill a 1½″-diameter hole through the front into the cavity under the round part of the note. Glue the tapered plug to the back of the note.

If you like more detail, burn a staff of five lines into the face of the bank; make sure the lines are straight and evenly spaced. This is best done with a soldering pencil and a straightedge. Sand the bank smooth and finish as desired.

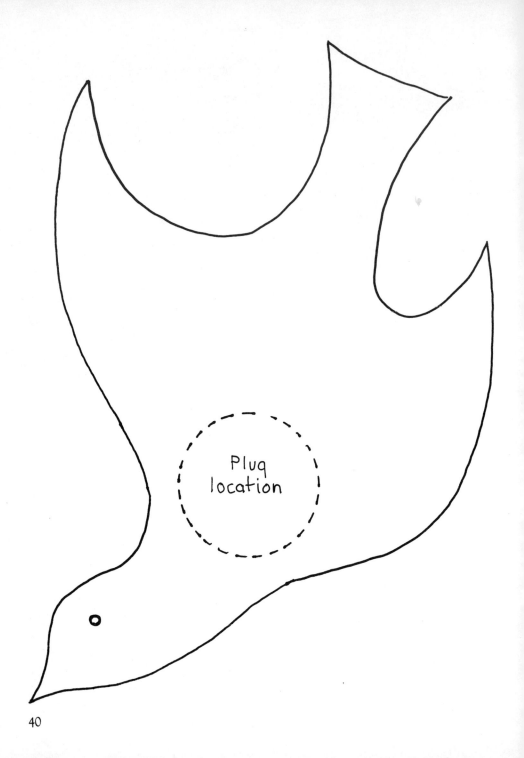

Plug
location

DOVE

The dove bank uses the same body as the flower bank, a ¾" × 5½" × 8½" hollow block. (See page 34.) Cut the dove out of a ½"-thick piece of wood. Use wood that will contrast with the body of the bank, such as pine with mahogany.

Sand the dove to make nicely rounded top edges or corners. The bottom edges should be left sharp. The sharp edge will sit tightly against the front surface, and the dove will appear to be glued on. Drill a 1½"-diameter hole under the dove for money removal. Make a 1½"-diameter plug with a slight taper and glue to the back of the dove. Sand the plug for a tight fit. Apply the finish of your choice.

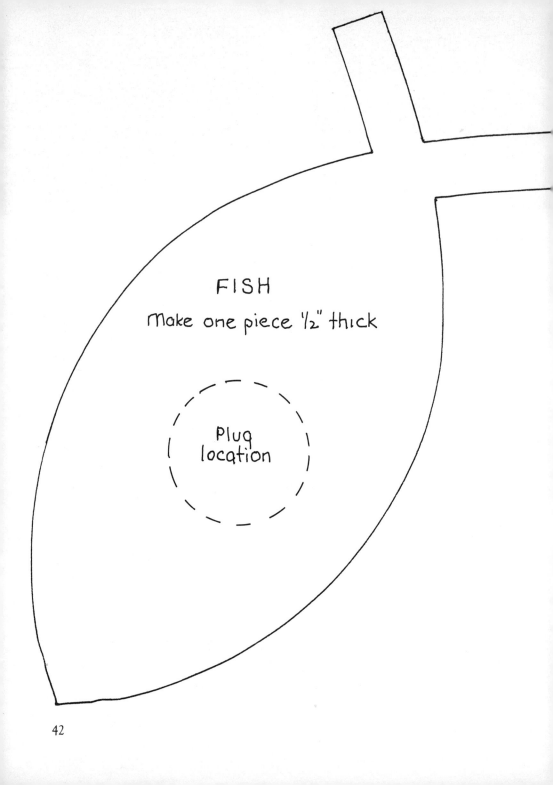

FISH

Make one piece ½" thick

Plug location

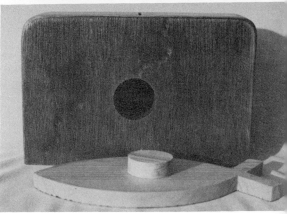

FISH

In the early days of the Christian church believers were often persecuted. To avoid trouble and to identify one another they would use the outline of a fish. This comes from the initial letters of "Jesus Christ, Son of God," which in Greek spell out the word for fish. A believer would scratch a curved line in the dirt. If the other person was also a believer he would scratch a second line completing the symbol. Today, the fish symbol on this bank is also found on plaques, lapel pins, and even bumper stickers.

 The fish bank is very simple to make. Use the body of the flower, but turn the block onto its side so it is 5½" high by 8½" long. (See page 34 for block pattern.) Cut the outline of the fish and sand the edges. The inside lines and letters can be drawn on or painted. If you want to try your hand at wood carving, incise them in the wood, making shallow "V"-cuts with a penknife. Woodburning is another idea for a nice finish. This can be done with a soldering pencil or iron. Drill a 1½"-diameter hole under the fish and make a tight-fitting plug. Glue it to the back of the fish. Finish as desired.

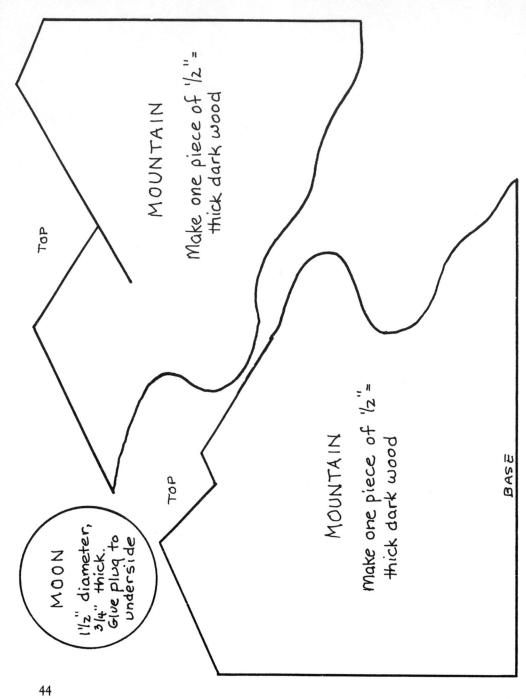

TOP

MOUNTAIN

Make one piece of 1/2" = thick dark wood

TOP

MOUNTAIN

Make one piece of 1/2" = thick dark wood

MOON
1 1/2" diameter, 3/4" thick. Give plug to underside

BASE

44

RIVER BANK
(pun intended)

For this bank use the same body as for the flower bank. (See pattern, page 34.) Make the face or front of a light-colored wood, the moon and mountain of darker pieces. The two mountain pieces are cut, sanded, and then glued to the front of the bank. The space between these pieces forms the river. Drill a 1½″-diameter hole in the sky for coin removal and to receive the moon plug. The plug is made of ¾″-thick wood and stands out approximately ½″ from the surface. Sand all edges and apply finish as desired.

Plug
location

SEA HORSE

This bank again uses the directions and body for the flower bank. (See page 34 for pattern.) Cut the sea horse of ½"-thick wood and sand all the edges round. Drill a ⅜"-diameter hole for the eye, ⅛" deep. The sea horse's mane and fin can be cut down by carving or whittling, it can be painted or stained a contrasting color, or the line can be burned in with a soldering pencil. Locate and drill a 1½"-diameter hole under the sea horse's belly for coin removal. Make a 1½"-diameter plug and glue it to the back of the sea horse's belly. Sand the entire bank, and apply a finish as desired.

Plug
location

48

STAMP

The body of this bank is once again the same as the flower bank. (See page 34 for pattern.) The size is a little smaller: 5½″ × 7¼″, to make the stamp more accurately proportioned. The center is composed of two pieces, ¾″ × 5½″ × 7¼″. The front and back are ½″ thick. Cut the tear holes around the edge of the front first, then glue on the front. If you wish, you can make the bank 1″ bigger in length and width and locate and drill ¾″-thick holes around the edge. Then saw through the middle of the holes to produce the stamp edge. Cut the eagle of ½″-thick wood and sand well. Wood-burn the design lines using a soldering pencil. Drill a 1½″-diameter hole under the eagle into the body of the bank. Make and glue a plug to the back of the eagle as with the other banks.

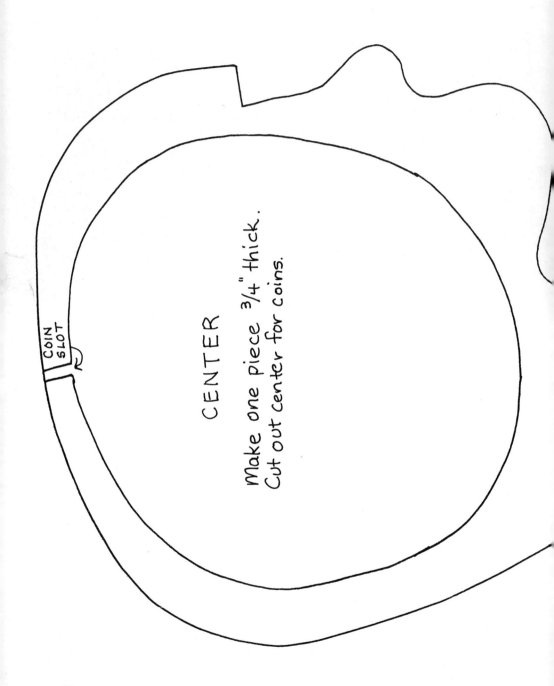

CENTER

Make one piece 3/4" thick.
Cut out center for coins.

COIN SLOT

50

FOOTBALL PLAYER

Lay out the parts on ¾"-thick wood. There are five parts that are ¾" thick; the two ear pieces are ½" thick. Carefully cut these parts to shape. Cut the middle out of the three center pieces to hold the coins. Glue the five head and helmet pieces together. Take care to line up the pieces; this will save much filing and sanding later. Drill a 1½"-diameter hole through the helmet under one of the ear pieces. Drill ¾"-diameter holes ⅛" deep in the center of each ear piece. Glue the ear piece to the helmet on the side without the 1½" hole. Make and glue a plug 1½" in diameter to the back of the other piece. Drill ½"-wide holes ⅛" deep for eyes. Make the face guard from automotive rubber tubing. Any gas station should be able to supply you with a short length. Press the tubing onto short dowels. Drill holes for the dowels in the helmet just in front of the ear pieces. File the corners round, and sand. Apply the finish of your choice.

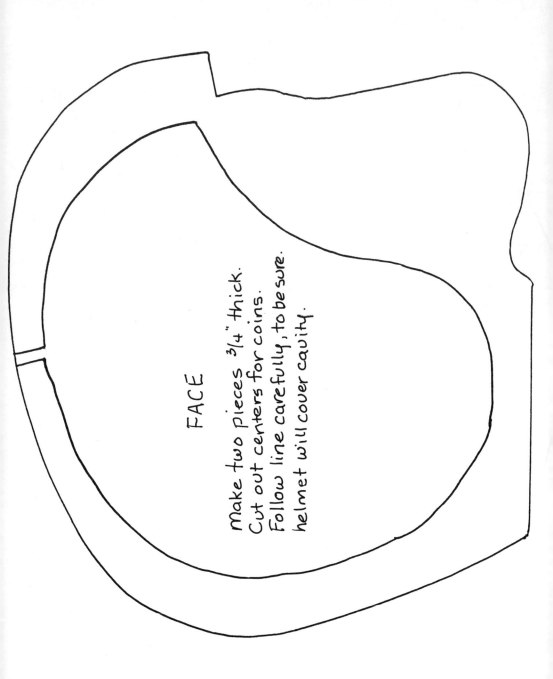

FACE

Make two pieces ³/₄" thick.
Cut out centers for coins.
Follow line carefully, to be sure.
helmet will cover cavity.

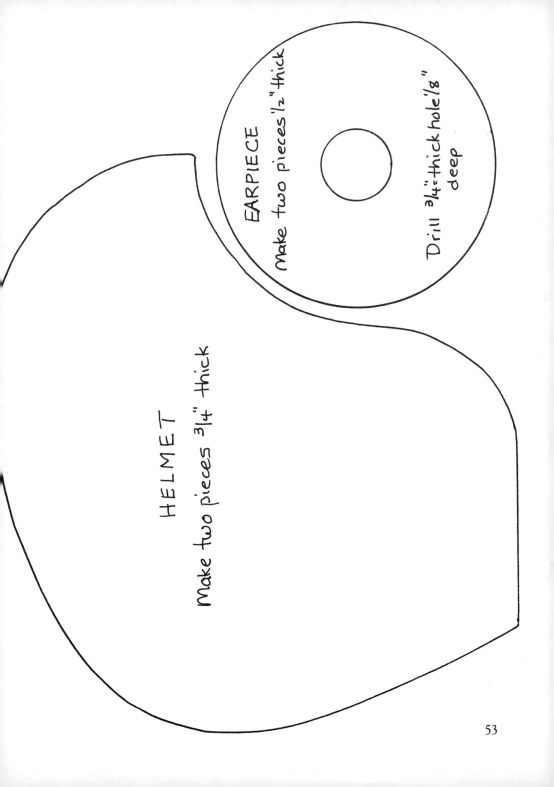

EARPIECE

Make two pieces ½" thick

Drill ¾" thick hole ⅛" deep

HELMET

Make two pieces ¾" thick

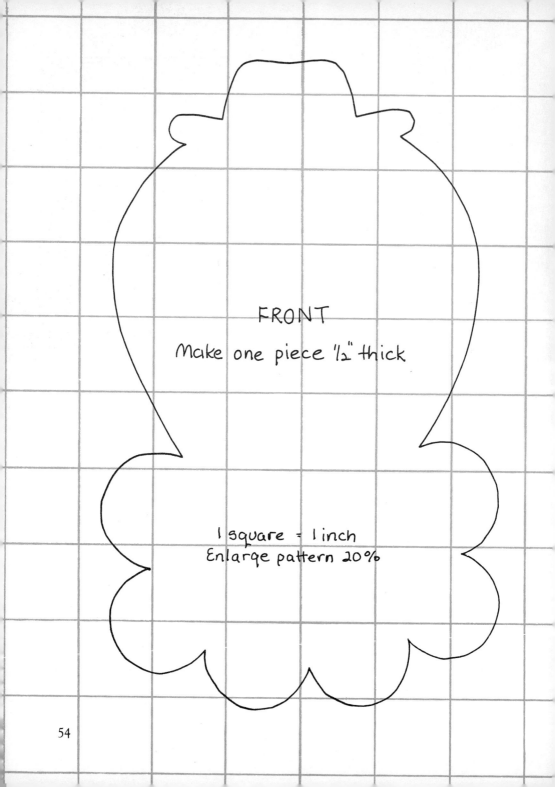

FRONT

Make one piece ½" thick

1 square = 1 inch
Enlarge pattern 20%

54

CLOWN

Lay out the parts and cut them to shape. Glue the two center sections together and saw out the middle, as is indicated by the dotted line, to receive and hold the coins. Glue the back to the two center pieces. File and sand the outside edges of this assembly to shape. Glue the front piece, eyes, mouth, and hat brim in place. File and sand the edges until round and smooth. Drill ½"-wide holes ⅛" deep for the eyes. Drill a 1¾" hole for the nose into cavity. Sand the nose (plug) to a slight 4° taper for a tight fit.

Use wood with contrasting colors to create the clown makeup appearance, or paint and/or stain to get the desired effect.

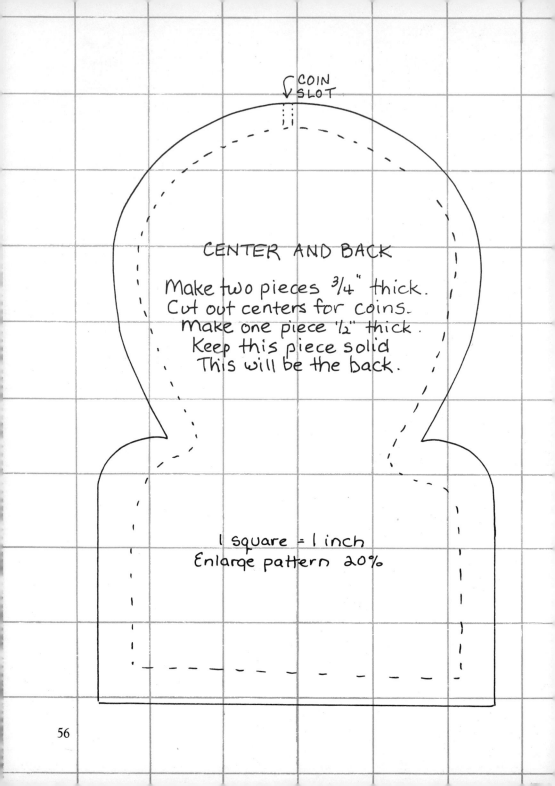

COIN
SLOT

CENTER AND BACK

Make two pieces ¾" thick.
Cut out centers for coins.
Make one piece ½" thick.
Keep this piece solid
This will be the back.

1 square = 1 inch
Enlarge pattern 20%

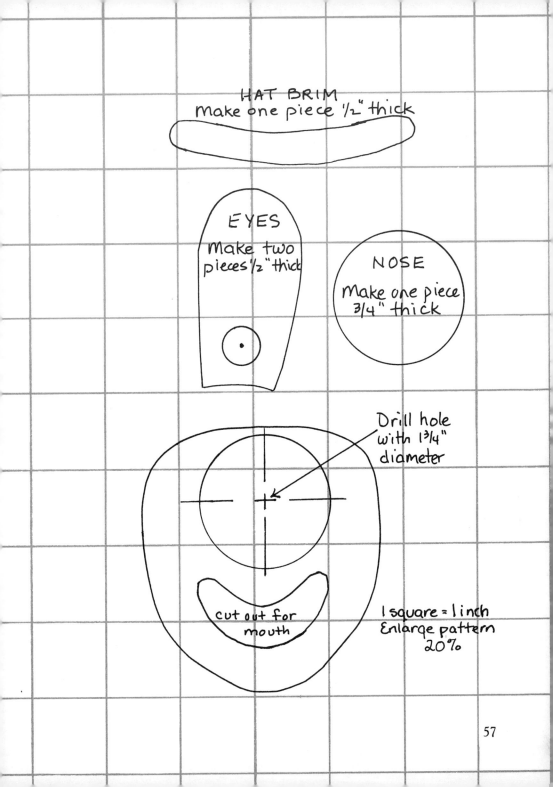

HAT BRIM
make one piece 1/2" thick

EYES
make two
pieces 1/2" thick

NOSE
make one piece
3/4" thick

Drill hole
with 1 3/4"
diameter

cut out for
mouth

1 square = 1 inch
Enlarge pattern
20%

57

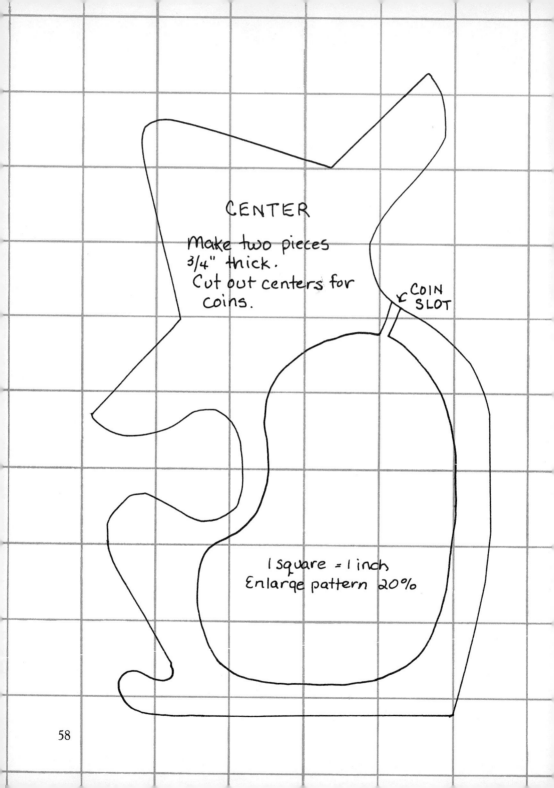

CENTER

Make two pieces
3/4" thick.
Cut out centers for
coins.

COIN
SLOT

1 square = 1 inch
Enlarge pattern 20%

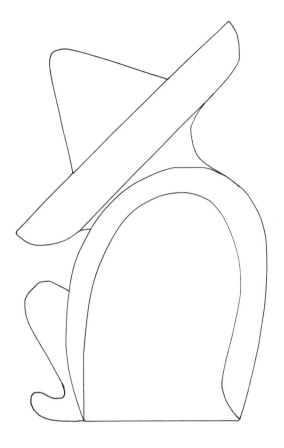

MEXICAN

Lay out the parts on the wood and cut them to shape. Glue the two center pieces together and cut out the inside for coins. Glue the hat brim pieces and the side pieces to the center section. When the glue has set, rasp, file, and sand this assembly to make the hat round. Glue and clamp the two side pieces to the center assembly. Drill a 1½"-diameter hole through one side. (Locate this hole so it will be covered by the outside "coat" piece.) Make a 1½"-diameter tapered plug, and glue it in position behind the outside piece. Glue the other outside piece to the other side. Round off the sharp edges with a file, and sand the bank thoroughly. Stain or paint bright colors as desired.

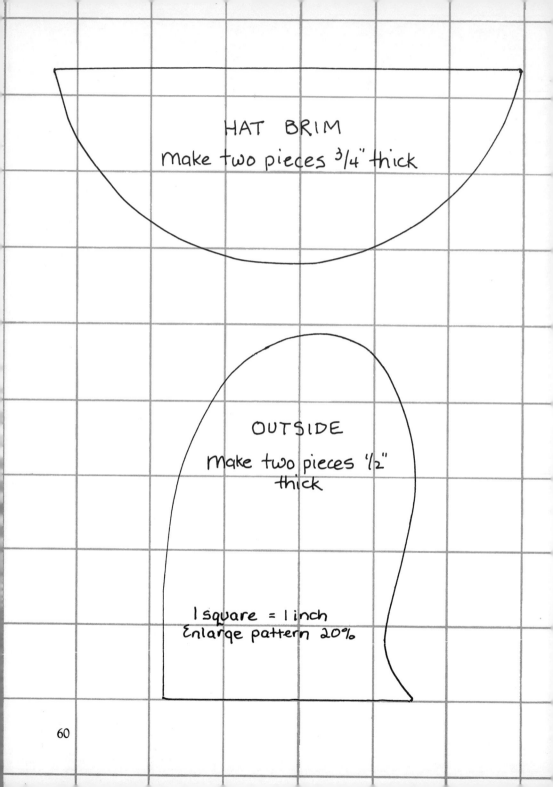

HAT BRIM
make two pieces 3/4" thick

OUTSIDE

make two pieces 1/2"
thick

1 square = 1 inch
Enlarge pattern 20%

60

SIDE

Make two pieces $\frac{1}{2}$" thick

Drill $1\frac{1}{2}$" diameter hole in one side for plug

PLUG
Make one piece $1\frac{1}{2}$" diameter, $\frac{1}{2}$" thick

1 square = 1 inch
Enlarge pattern 20%

61

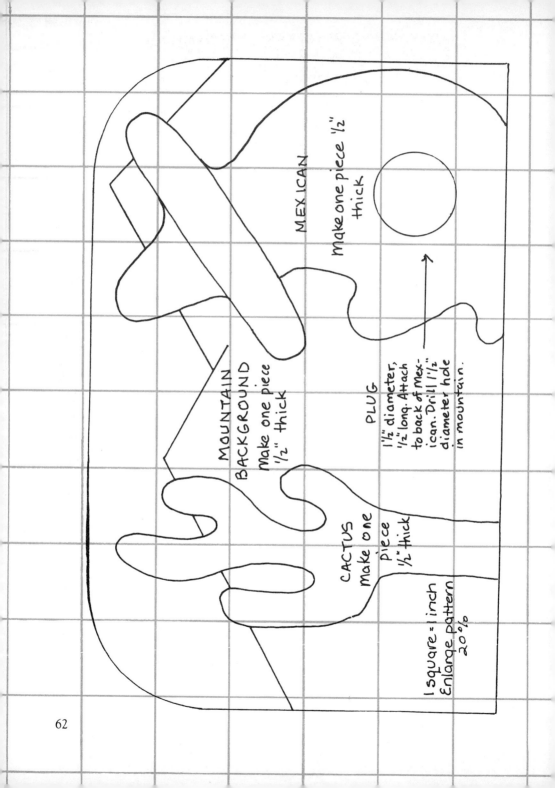

MEXICAN

Make one piece ½" thick

MOUNTAIN
BACKGROUND
make one piece
½" thick

PLUG

1½" diameter,
½" long. Attach
to back of Mex-
ican. Drill 1½"
diameter hole
in mountain.

CACTUS
make one
piece
½" thick

1 square = 1 inch
Enlarge pattern
20%

62

MEXICAN SCENE

Make the body for this bank using the directions for the flower bank, only it is on its side like the fish and river banks. Use two pieces ¾" × 5½" × 8½" glued together, with the center cut out for coins. (See page 34 for pattern.) Glue two pieces ½" × 5½" × 8½" onto the front and back. Cut the mountain piece to shape, and glue it onto the front. Drill a 1½"-diameter hole into the coin cavity under the Mexican. Cut out the cactus and the Mexican from ½"-thick wood and sand the edges smooth. Glue the cactus to the front. Make a 1½"-diameter plug and glue it to the back of the Mexican. Sand the entire bank and apply finish as desired.

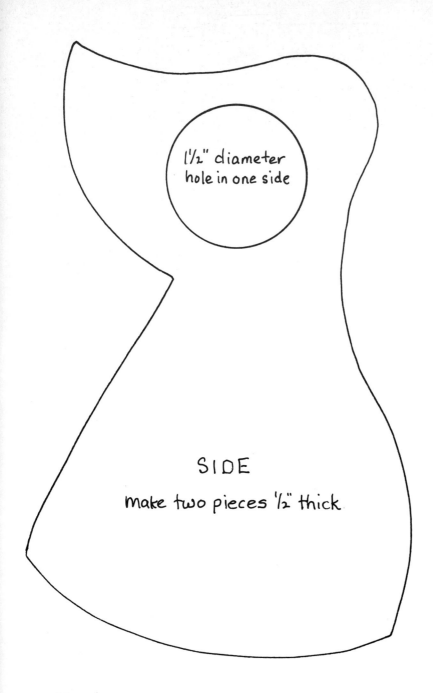

1½" diameter hole in one side

SIDE

make two pieces ½" thick

BONNET DOLL

This entire bank is made from ½"-thick wood. Lay out the parts on the wood and cut them to shape. Glue the three middle parts together and cut out the center for coins. Glue the sides to the center assembly. Glue the bonnet to one side. Drill a 1½"-diameter hole under the bonnet on the other side. Make the plug with a 4° taper and glue it to the underside of the bonnet piece. With the bonnet piece pressed into place, file and sand all the edges, rounding the corners. Sand the arms and glue them into place on the sides. Apply finish as desired.

PLUG
½" thick

BONNET
Make two pieces ½" thick

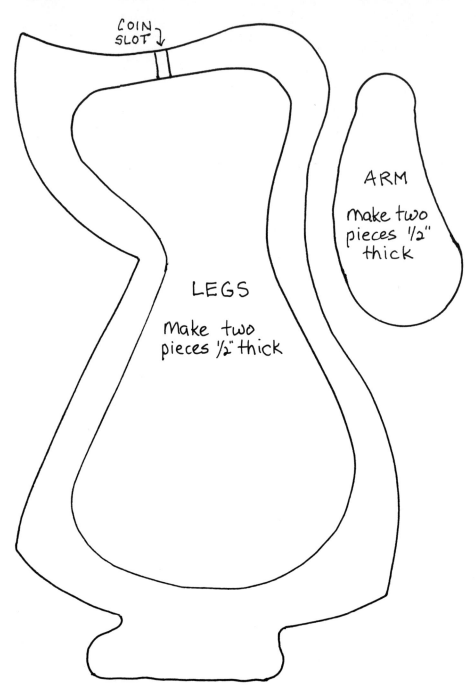

COIN
SLOT ↓

ARM

make two
pieces 1/2"
thick

LEGS

Make two
pieces 1/2" thick

66

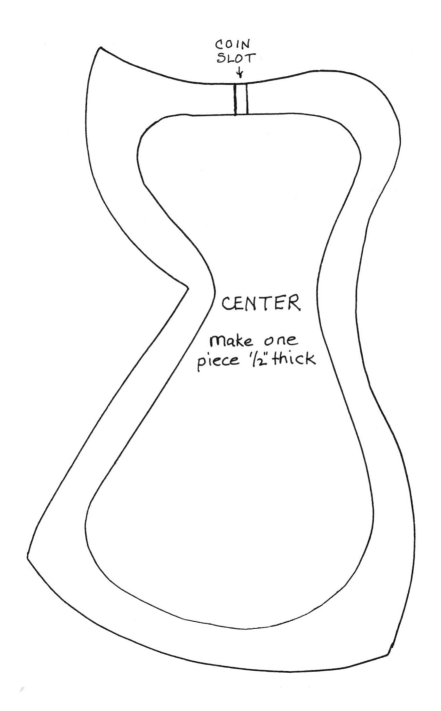

COIN
SLOT
↓

CENTER

make one
piece 1/2" thick

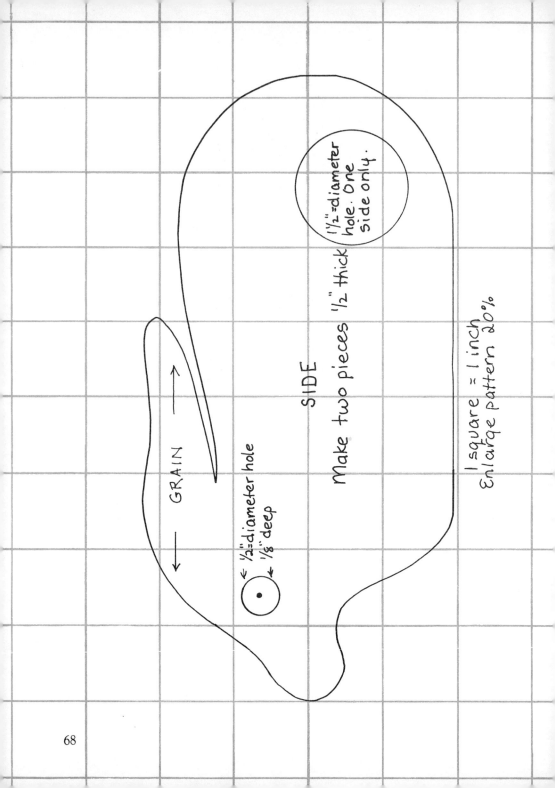

GRAIN

1/2"=diameter hole
1/8" deep

SIDE

Make two pieces 1/2" thick

1 1/2"=diameter hole. One side only.

1 square = 1 inch
Enlarge pattern 20%

68

BUNNY

All the parts for this bank are made from ½″-thick wood. Lay out the parts and cut them to shape. Note the direction of the grain on the ears and legs. Glue the three middle pieces together, tail in the center, to make a 1½″-thick block. Cut out the middle for coins. Make a ⅛″-wide coin slot between the ears and sand at this time, as it is quite difficult to sand when the sides are glued on. Glue the sides to the middle section. Drill ½″ holes ⅛″ deep for eyes. Drill a 1½″-diameter hole under one rear leg and glue the plug to the underside of this leg. Glue the three other legs to the body. Rasp all the corners round. Taper the nose towards the middle. Sand until smooth. Finish as desired.

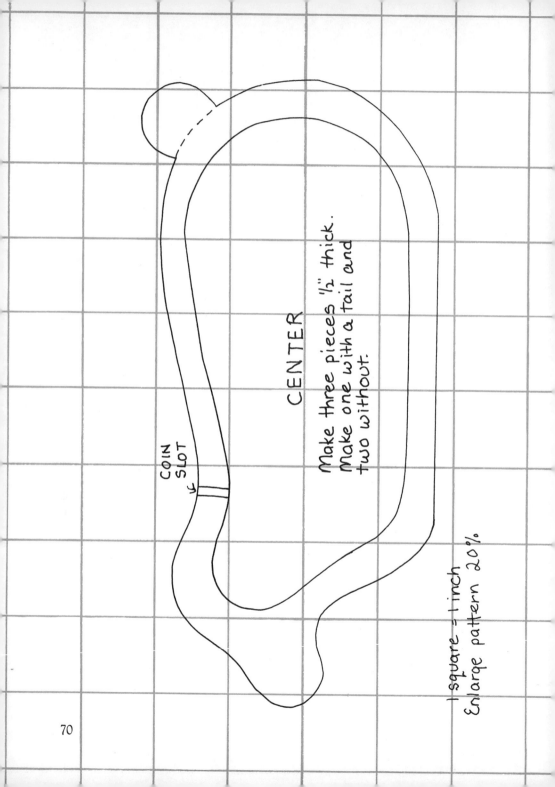

COIN
SLOT

CENTER

Make three pieces 1/2" thick.
Make one with a tail and
two without.

1 square = 1 inch
Enlarge pattern 20%

70

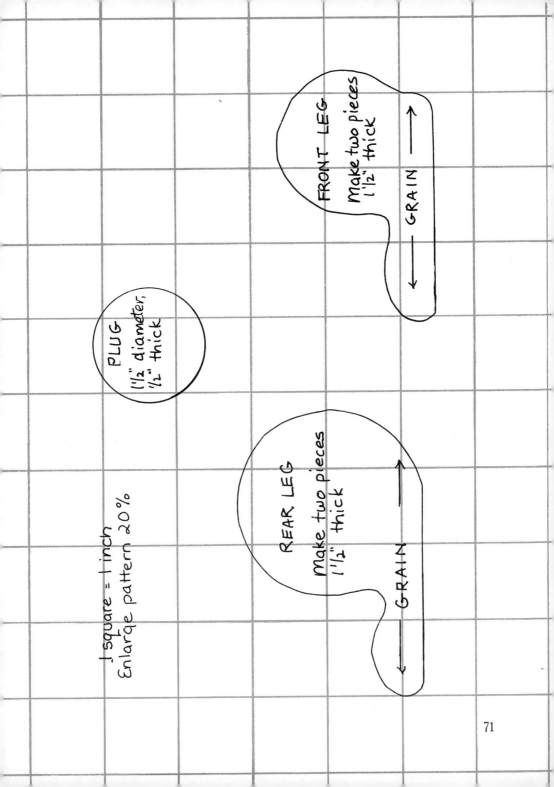

FRONT LEG

Make two pieces
1½" thick

← GRAIN →

PLUG
1½" diameter,
½" thick

REAR LEG

Make two pieces
1½" thick

← GRAIN →

1 square = 1 inch
Enlarge pattern 20%

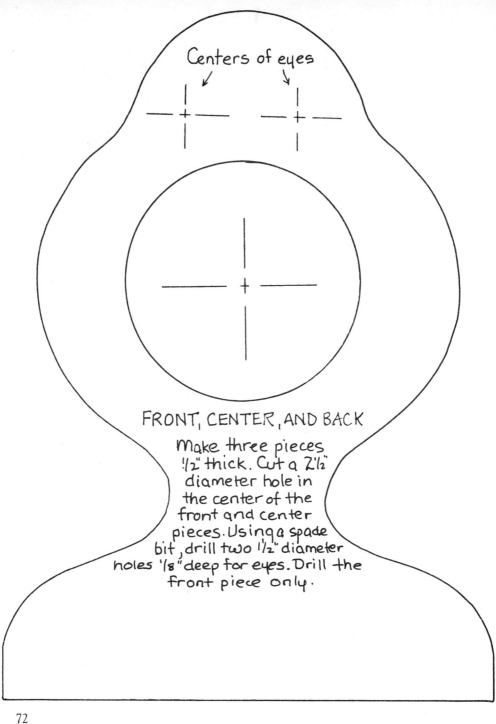

Centers of eyes

FRONT, CENTER, AND BACK

Make three pieces
1/2" thick. Cut a 2 1/2"
diameter hole in
the center of the
front and center
pieces. Using a spade
bit, drill two 1/2" diameter
holes 1/8" deep for eyes. Drill the
front piece only.

MOOSE

Lay out the pattern for the moose on ½"-thick wood. Make the nose and antlers of dark wood, such as mahogany, and the rest of a lighter-colored wood, such as pine. Drill out the middle of each piece with a 2½"-diameter hole saw, or use a coping saw before sawing the outline to shape; this will reduce the chance of breaking the pieces. When the pieces are cut to shape, glue the head pieces together. Align carefully, to avoid filing and sanding later. The antlers and corresponding head piece are located next to the back. The antlers should be the same thickness or made from the same piece of wood as the head piece below them. This will make a tight fit for the removable antlers. When glueing the head pieces be careful to remove all excess glue from the slot the antlers will fit into as it is difficult to remove it later.

Drill or cut out the center of two of the nose pieces; then cut the outside to shape. Glue the three nose pieces together offsetting each a little to create a long, drooping nose. When dry, rasp, file, and sand the nose to remove all corners or sharp edges. Glue the nose into place on the head. Make two saw cuts ⅛" deep on the dotted lines of the antlers. Remove the wood between these cuts to make the coin slot. You can make a number of saw cuts ⅛" deep in the middle to help remove the wood but keep the slot 1½" wide.

Drill holes ½" × ⅛" deep for eyes and ⅜" × ⅛" deep for the nostrils. Apply finish as desired.

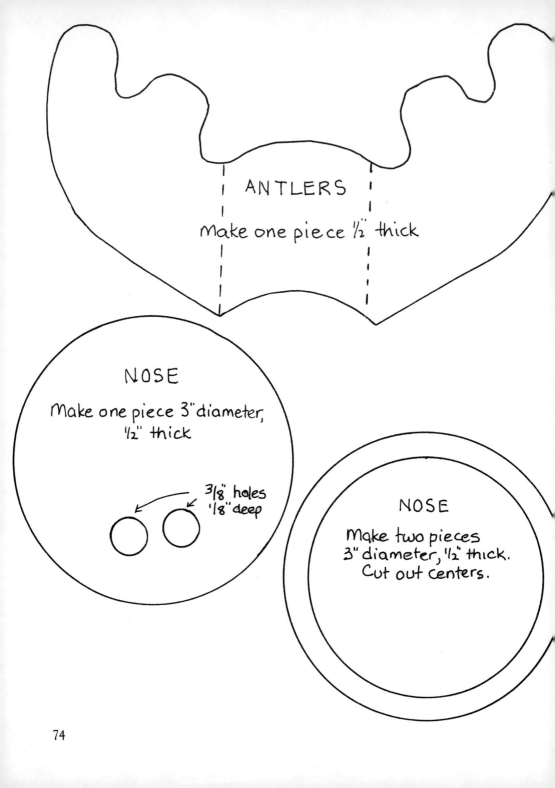

ANTLERS

Make one piece ½" thick

NOSE

Make one piece 3" diameter,
½" thick

3/8" holes
1/8" deep

NOSE

Make two pieces
3" diameter, ½" thick.
Cut out centers.

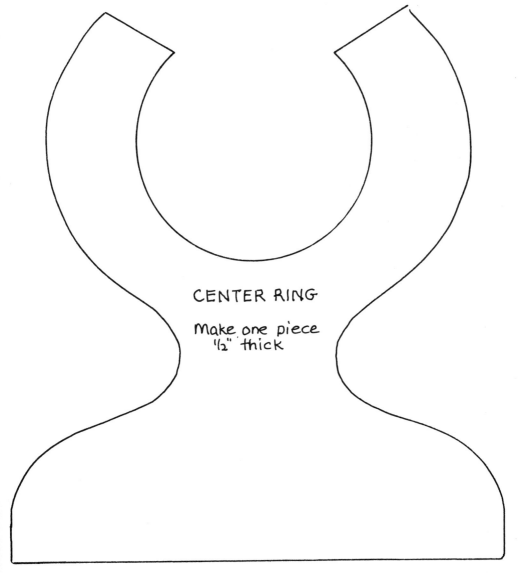

CENTER RING

Make one piece
½" thick

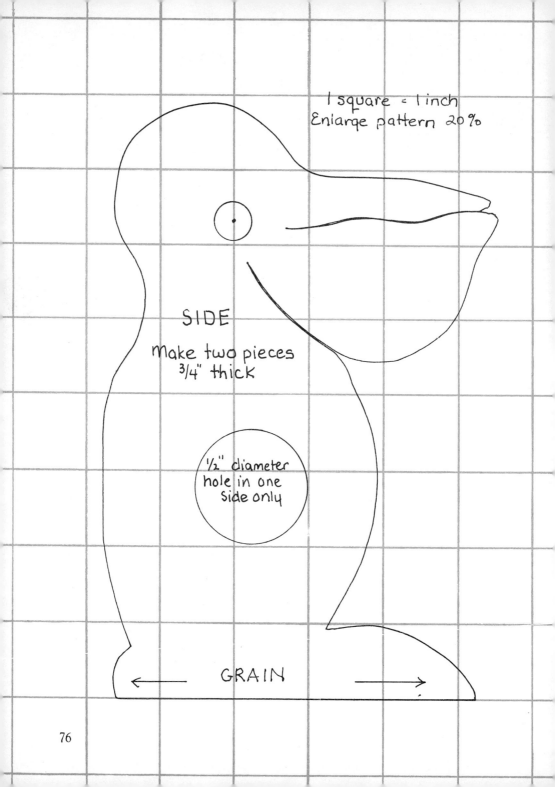

1 square = 1 inch
Enlarge pattern 20%

SIDE

Make two pieces
3/4" thick

1/2" diameter
hole in one
Side only

GRAIN

PELICAN

Lay out the parts on ¾″ thick wood. Pay attention to the direction of the grain for maximum strength. If the inside and outside pieces have the grain at 90° angles the bank will be strong. Cut the inside of the middle pieces first. Leave some wood uncut under the chin for strength. Cut the pieces to shape. Glue the four body pieces together. When the glue has set, carefully cut the mouth slot and under the chin. Note that the long coin slot in the lower bill of the two center pieces must be straight for coins to slide down the pelican's throat. Try some quarters and nickels before glueing the sides. Drill ½″-wide holes ⅛″ deep for the eyes and a 1½″-diameter hole under one of the wings. Make a 1½″-diameter plug ½″ thick with a 4° taper to fit tightly into this hole. Glue the plug to the back of the wing. Glue the other wing in place on the other side of the bank. Rasp, file, and sand all the edges round and smooth. Apply the finish of yor choice.

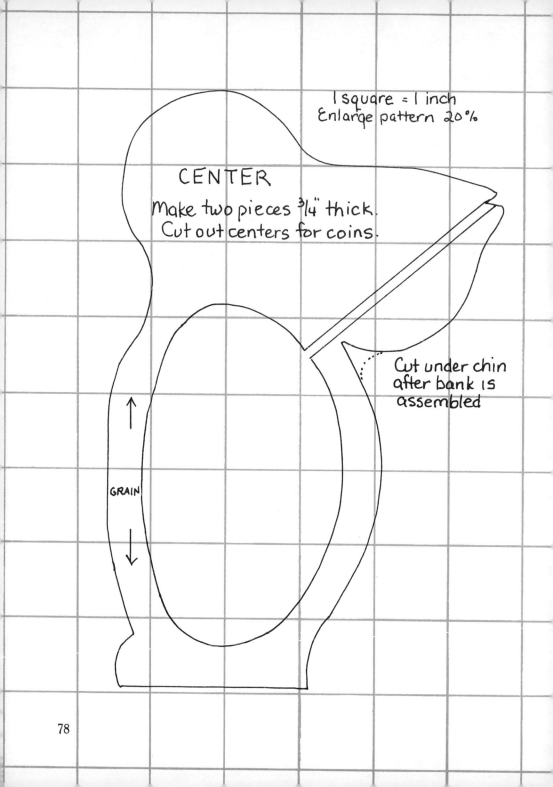

1 square = 1 inch
Enlarge pattern 20%

CENTER

Make two pieces ¾" thick.
Cut out centers for coins.

GRAIN

Cut under chin
after bank is
assembled

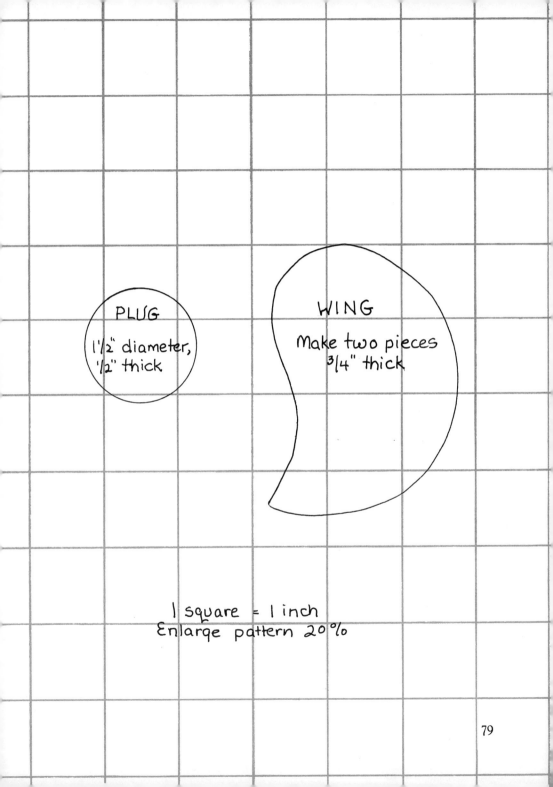

PLUG

1½" diameter,
½" thick

WING

Make two pieces
¾" thick

1 square = 1 inch
Enlarge pattern 20%

79

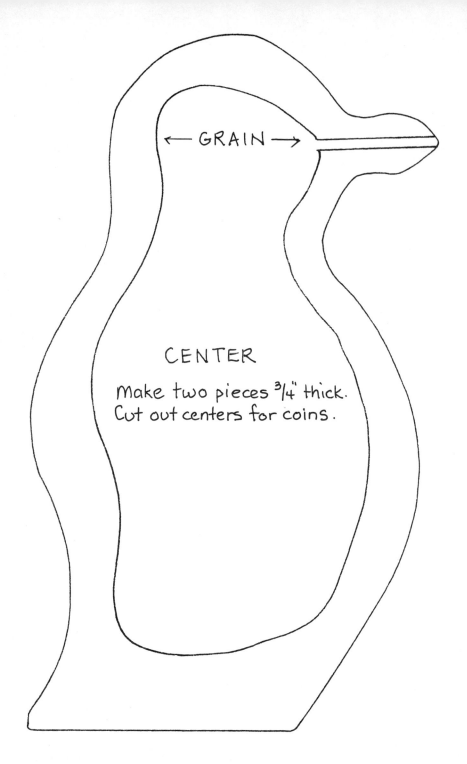

← GRAIN →

CENTER

Make two pieces ³/₄" thick.
Cut out centers for coins.

PENGUIN

To obtain the penguin-look, this bank has to be made from contrasting colored woods. Use pine and mahogany or woods with similar colors. The coat and wings should be dark and ½"-thick wood. The side pieces with legs are a light color ½" thick. The two center pieces are light and ¾" thick. Lay out the parts and cut to shape. Glue the body parts together. Be careful to align the bill (beak) so coins will slide through. Smooth the front part of the coat before glueing. Drill holes for eyes. Drill a 1½"-diameter plug to back of one wing. Glue the other wing to the other side of the penguin. Rasp, file, and sand the bank to shape. Round all corners and sharp edges. Finish as desired.

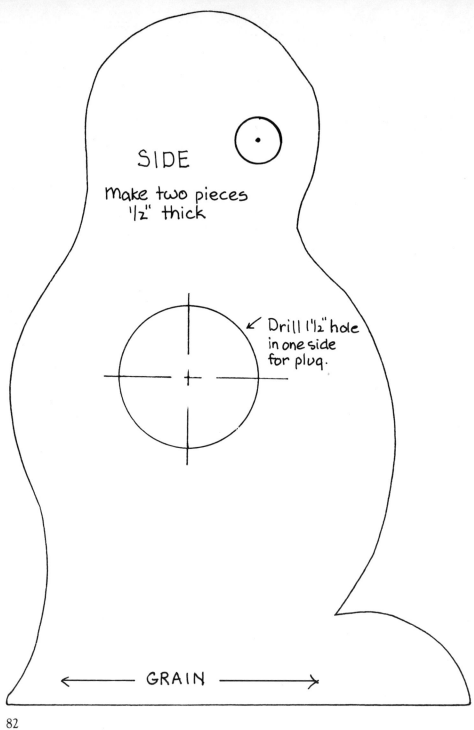

SIDE

make two pieces
$\frac{1}{2}$" thick

← Drill $1\frac{1}{2}$" hole
in one side
for plug.

← GRAIN →

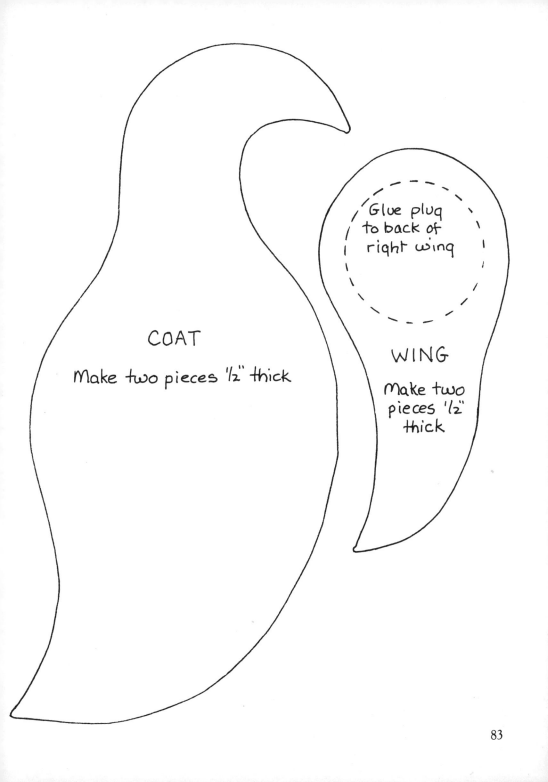

COAT

Make two pieces 1/2" thick

Glue plug
to back of
right wing

WING

Make two
pieces 1/2"
thick

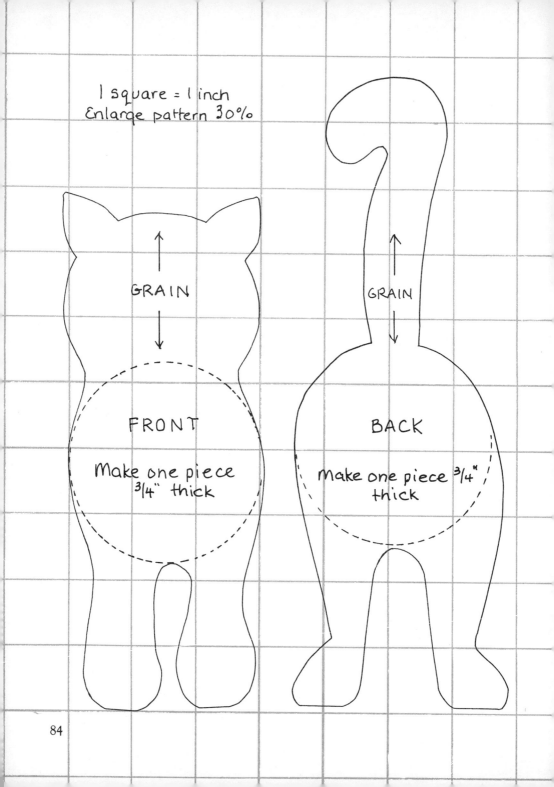

1 square = 1 inch
Enlarge pattern 30%

GRAIN

FRONT

Make one piece
3/4" thick

GRAIN

BACK

Make one piece 3/4"
thick

CAT

Lay out the front and back of the cat on ¾″ wood. Note the direction of the grain on these pieces. The body is made from six rings cut from ¾″-thick wood. The outside of the ring is a 3″-diameter circle. The center hole has a 2″ diameter. Lay out these rings on the wood and use a 2″-diameter hole saw to drill out the inside. With the inside drilled out, cut the outside to shape. Glue two rings together, and when the glue has set, cut a ⅛″-wide coin slot across the side of these two rings into the center hole. Glue two rings on either side of these, to form a 4½″-long cylinder. Make a ½″-thick plug with a 2″-diameter. Taper slightly to fit tightly into one end of the cylinder. Glue this plug to either the front or back of the cat. Glue the other piece (front or back) to the cylinder. Rasp, file, and sand until all edges are round and smooth. Use a soldering pencil to burn eyes, nose, mouth, and whiskers into face. Finish as desired.

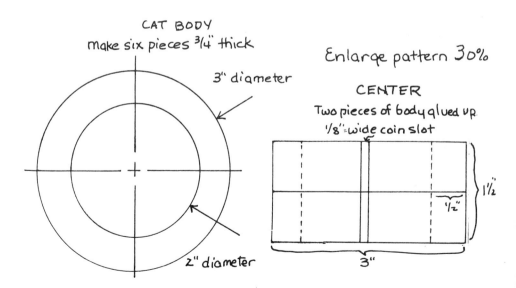

CAT BODY
make six pieces ¾″ thick

3″ diameter

2″ diameter

Enlarge pattern 30%

CENTER
Two pieces of body glued up
⅛″-wide coin slot

1½″

½″

3″

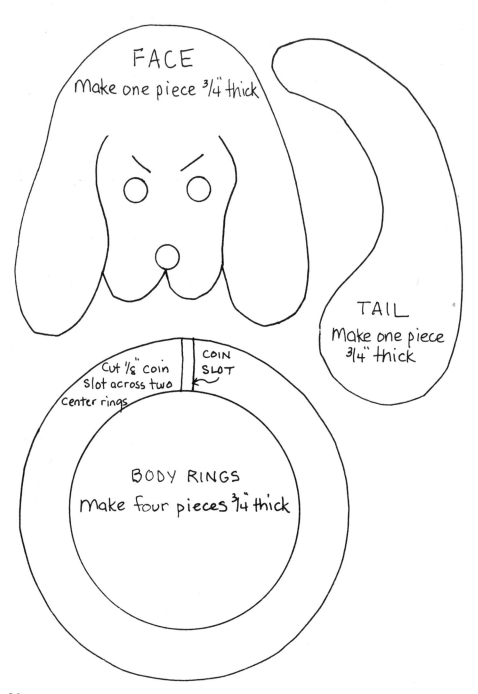

FACE
Make one piece ³/₄" thick

TAIL
Make one piece
³/₄" thick

Cut ⅛" coin
slot across two
center rings

COIN
SLOT

BODY RINGS
Make four pieces ³/₄" thick

DOG

Lay out the parts on ¾"-thick wood. Drill the center hole in the body parts (rings) using a 2½"-hole saw; then cut the parts out to shape. Glue two of the body rings together and when dry cut a slot ⅛" wide by 1½" long through the top of these two rings into the center. Glue a ring on each side of these rings to make the body cylinder. Glue the back to the body and the tail to the back. Glue the face to the front. Drill ¼"-diameter holes ⅛" deep for the eyes and nose. Carve or burn lines for ears and eyebrows. Make a 2½"-diameter tapered plug and glue to the back of the front piece to fit tightly into hole on the front of the body. Rasp, file and sand until the dog is smooth and all the edges are round. Finish as desired.

The face and tail can be attached with ¾" dowels, and cut 1" long. Drill a blind hole (not all the way through) into the surface of each piece. Tap the dowel into the hole and the piece onto the dowel. This way the head and tail will be movable.

BACK

Make one piece 3/4" thick

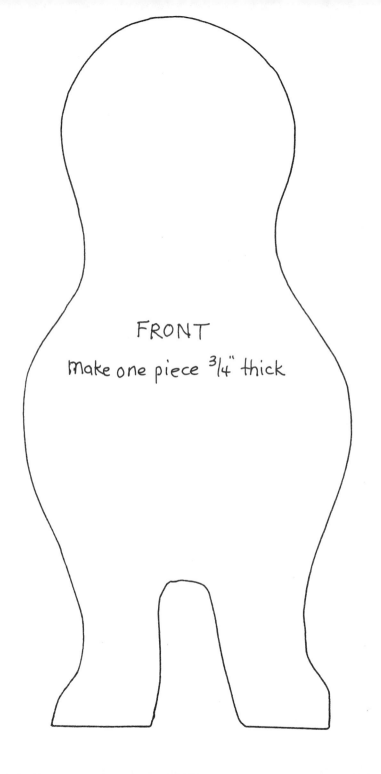

FRONT

make one piece ³/₄" thick

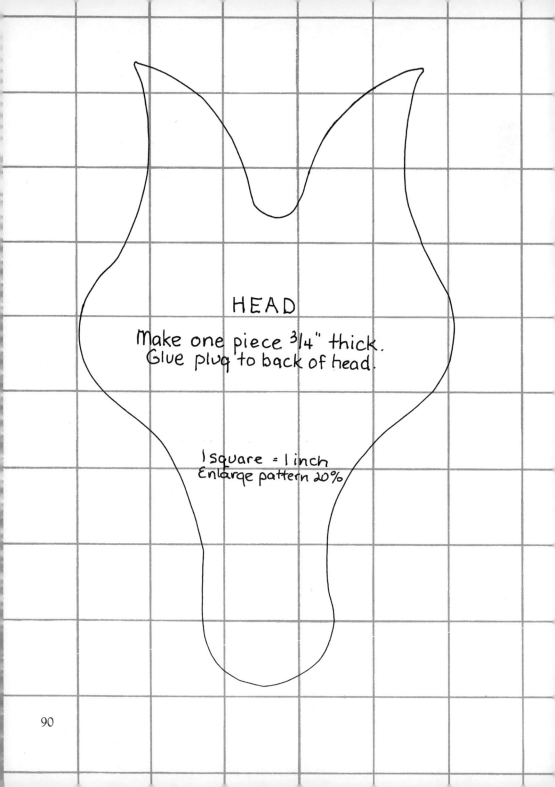

HEAD

Make one piece 3/4" thick.
Glue plug to back of head.

1 square = 1 inch
Enlarge pattern 20%

MR. FOX

Lay out the parts on ¾"-thick wood and cut to shape. The body (ring) parts are 3½"-diameter circles with a 2½" hole in the middle. There will be less chance of breakage if the holes are cut before the outside. Glue two rings together and cut a ⅛"-wide coin slot through the top into the center. Glue a ring on each side of these two rings. Glue the two face pieces together. Drill the eyes ⅛" deep using a ½" spade bit. The head must be well-rounded. Use a rasp, file, and sandpaper to remove all sharpness. Drill a 1½"-diameter hole through the top of the piece forming the front legs. Taper a 1½"-diameter plug to fit tightly in this hole. Glue the plug to the neck piece and the neck to the back of the head.

The tail can be glued to the back-leg piece or held with a ¾" dowel in two blind holes, if you wish the tail to move. Glue the leg pieces to the body. File and sand all edges smooth and round. Finish as desired.

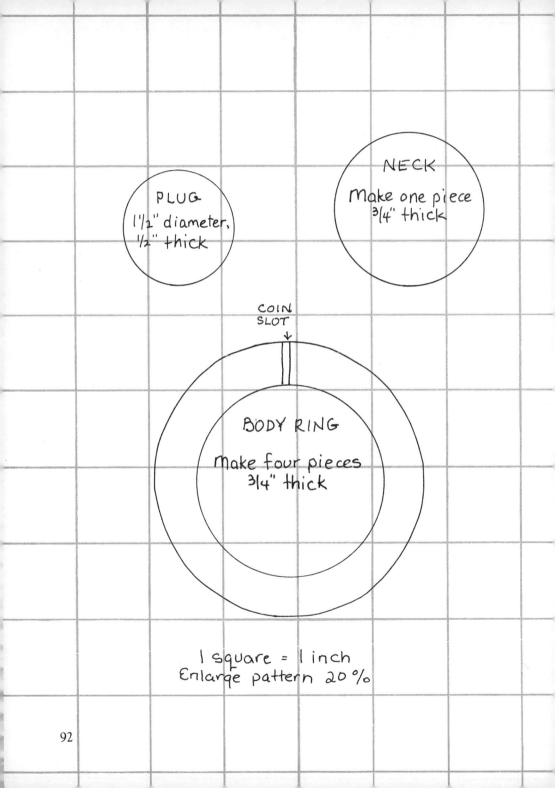

PLUG

1½" diameter,
½" thick

NECK

Make one piece
¾" thick

COIN
SLOT
↓

BODY RING

Make four pieces
¾" thick

1 square = 1 inch
Enlarge pattern 20%

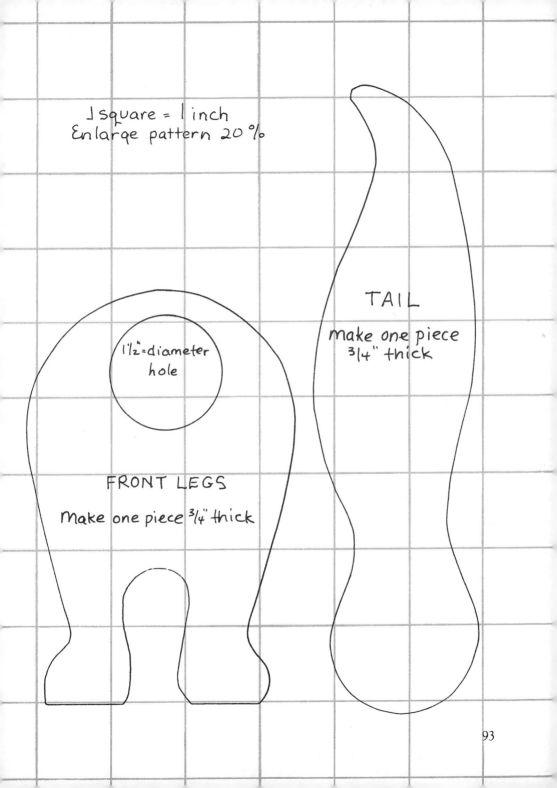

1 square = 1 inch
Enlarge pattern 20%

TAIL

make one piece
3/4" thick

1½"=diameter
hole

FRONT LEGS

Make one piece 3/4" thick

93

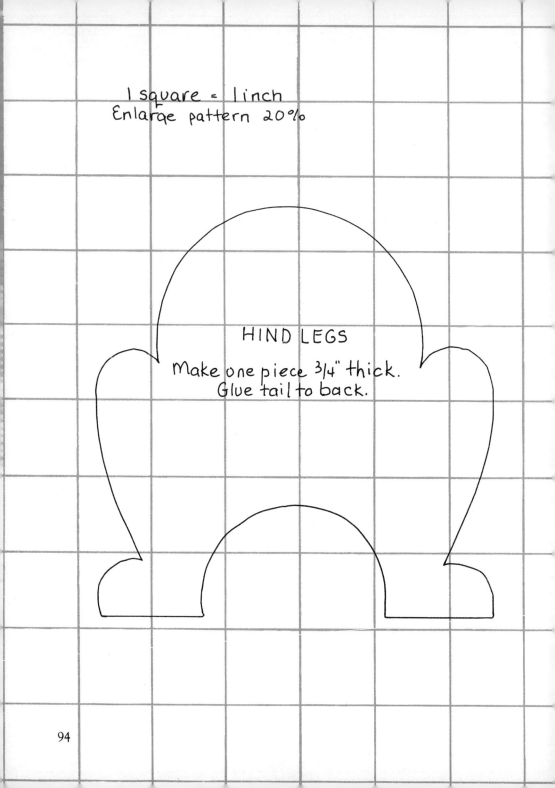

1 square = 1 inch
Enlarge pattern 20%

HIND LEGS

Make one piece 3/4" thick.
Glue tail to back.

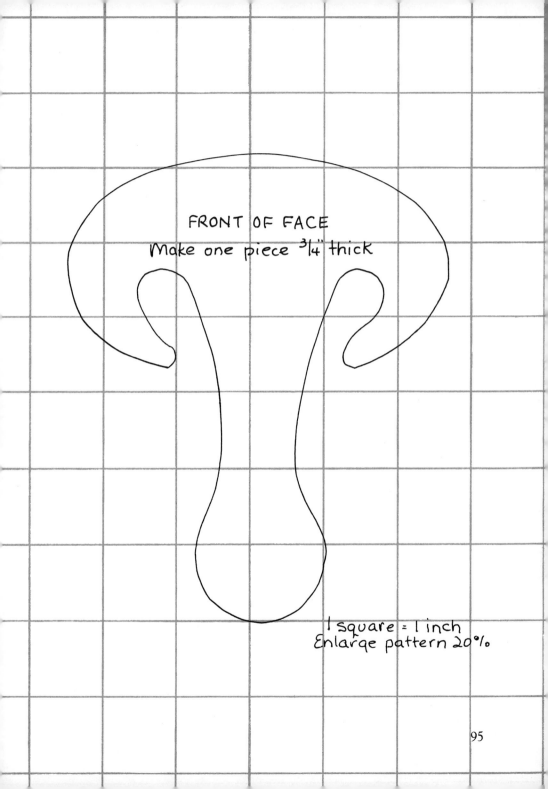

FRONT OF FACE
Make one piece ³⁄₄" thick

1 square = 1 inch
Enlarge pattern 20%

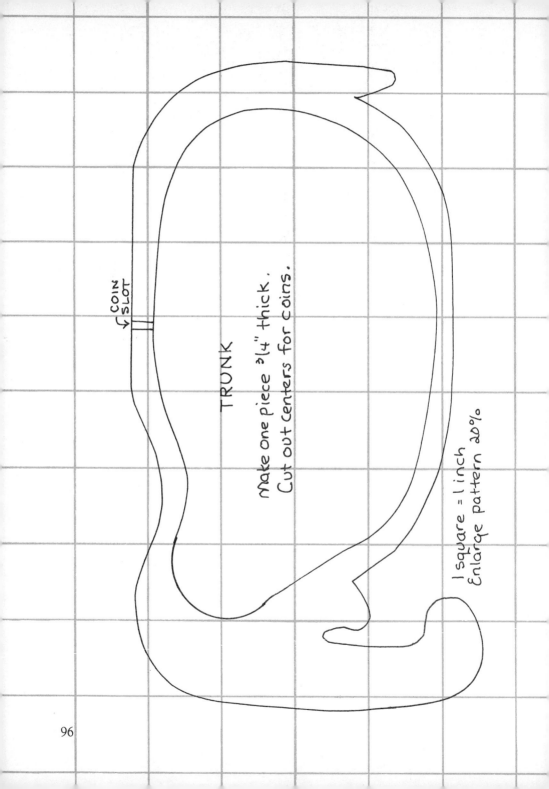

COIN
SLOT

TRUNK

Make one piece 3/4" thick.
Cut out centers for coins.

1 square = 1 inch
Enlarge pattern 20%

ELEPHANT BANK ONE

Lay out the parts on ¾"-thick wood and cut them to shape. The trunk and legs should be filed and sanded round and smooth before assembly. Drill holes under the location of the ears. Make two 1½"-diameter tapered plugs to fit tightly into these holes and glue them to the back of the ears. Drill ¼" holes to hold ¼" × 1½"-long dowels for tusks. Glue the parts together. File and sand all edges round and smooth. Apply finish as desired.

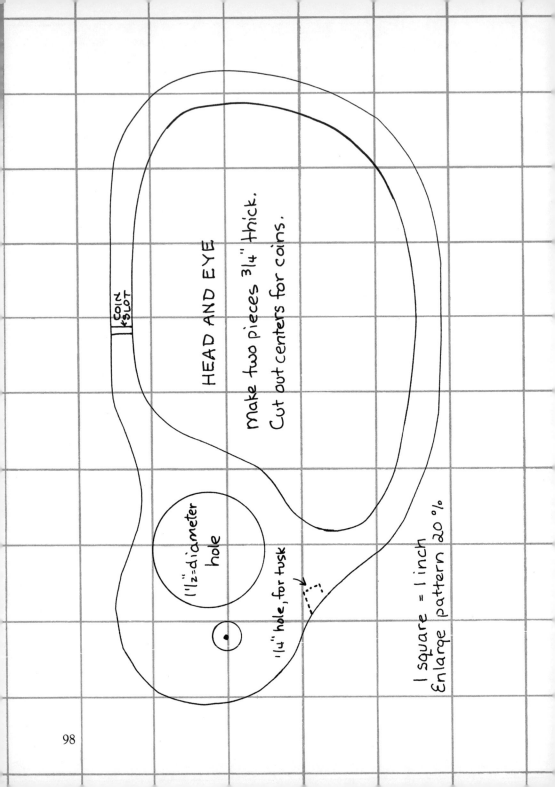

COIN SLOT

HEAD AND EYE

Make two pieces 3|4" thick.
Cut out centers for coins.

1'1/2"-diameter hole

1|4" hole, for tusk

1 square = 1 inch
Enlarge pattern 20%

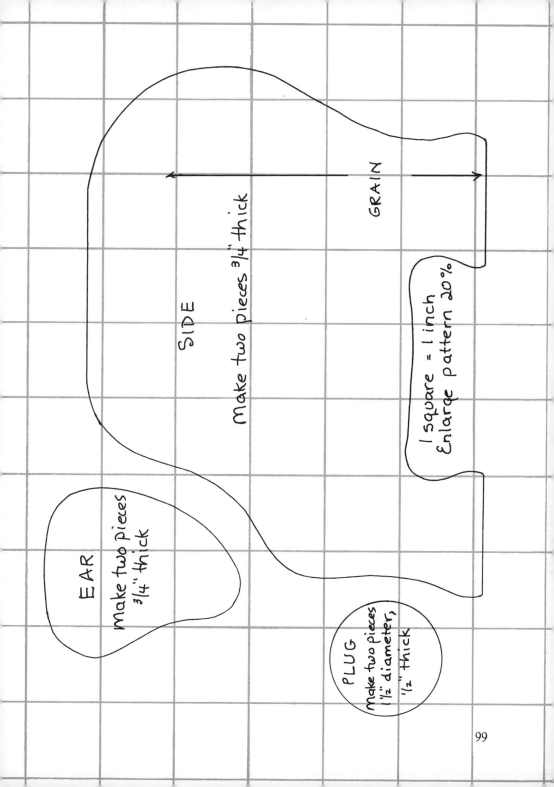

SIDE

Make two pieces 3/4" thick

GRAIN

1 square = 1 inch
Enlarge pattern 20%

EAR

Make two pieces
3/4" thick

PLUG

Make two pieces
1½" diameter,
½" thick

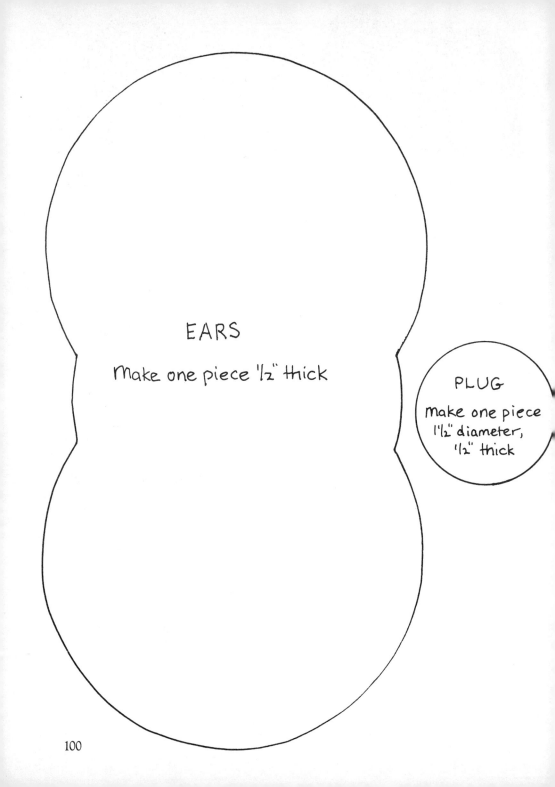

EARS

make one piece '/2" thick

PLUG

make one piece
1'/2" diameter,
'/2" thick

ELEPHANT BANK TWO

The construction of this bank is similar to that of the cat, dog, and fox. Lay out the ears on ½"-thick wood. The other parts are ¾" thick. Cut the parts to shape. Glue two of the body rings together and when dry cut a ⅛"-wide coin slot through the top into the center. Glue a ring on each side of these two rings, and glue the legs on each end of the body. Drill ½"-wide holes ⅛" deep for the eyes. Drill ¼"-wide holes at a slight angle for the tusks. Glue ¼" dowels into these holes about 1½" long. Glue the trunk to the face between eyes and tusks. Glue the face to the ears. Make the 1½"-tapered plug fit the hole in the front and glue it to the back of the ears. File and sand all edges round and smooth. If a tail is desired, drill a hole and glue a short piece of rope into it. Finish as desired.

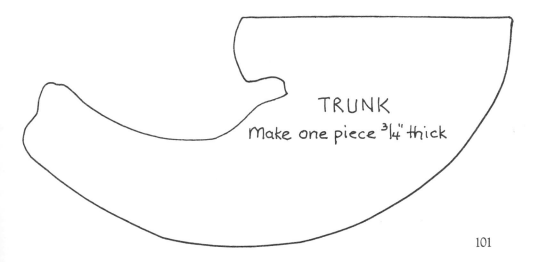

TRUNK
Make one piece ¾" thick

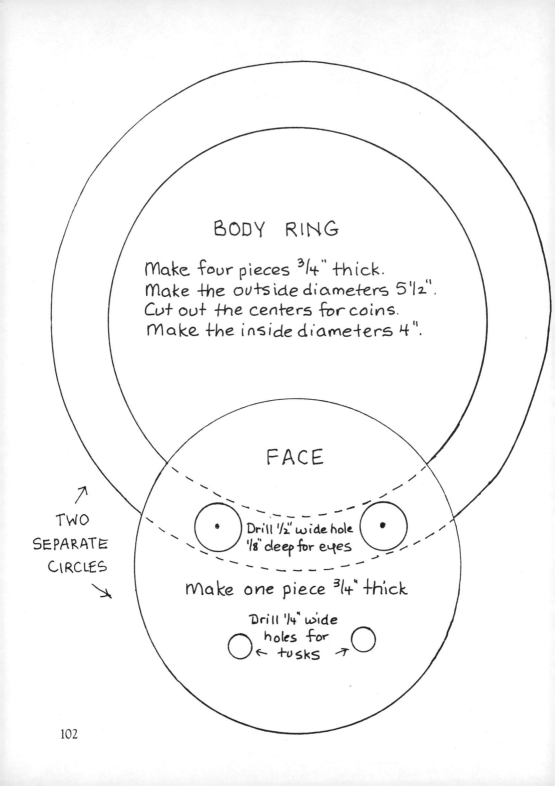

BODY RING

Make four pieces $3/4$" thick.
Make the outside diameters $5 1/2$".
Cut out the centers for coins.
Make the inside diameters 4".

FACE

Drill $1/2$" wide hole
$1/8$" deep for eyes

TWO
SEPARATE
CIRCLES

Make one piece $3/4$" thick

Drill $1/4$" wide
holes for
← tusks →

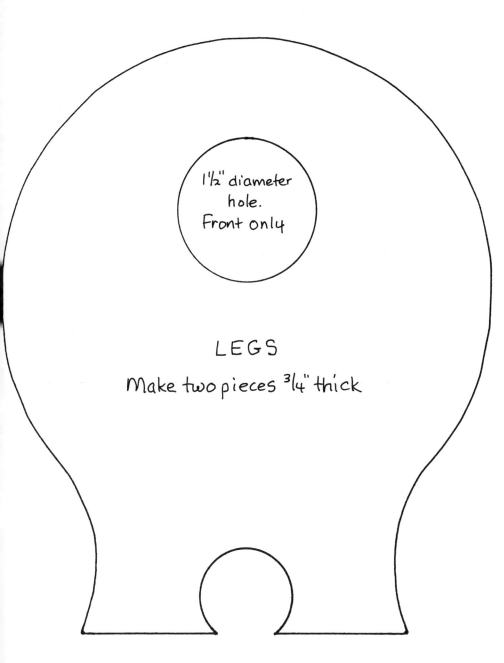

1½" diameter
hole.
Front only

LEGS

Make two pieces ¾" thick

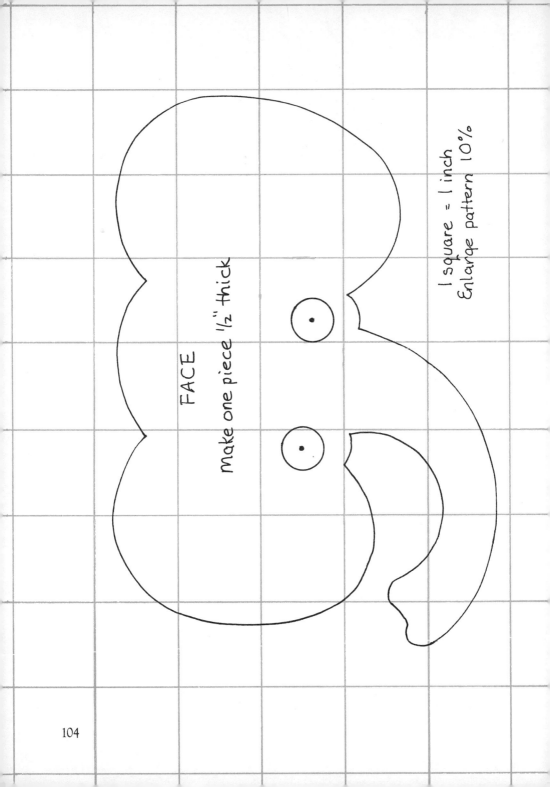

FACE
Make one piece 1/2" thick

1 square = 1 inch
Enlarge pattern 10%

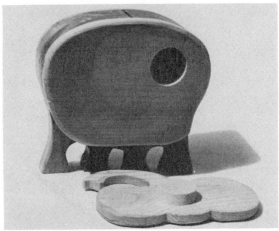

ELEPHANT BANK THREE

Lay out the face, front, and back on ½"-thick wood. Lay out the leg and body pieces on ¾"-thick stock. Cut all the parts to shape. Glue the two ¾"-thick body pieces together and cut a ⅛"-wide coin slot across the top into the center cavity. Glue the leg pieces on front and back so that one set is to the left and the other to the right. Glue ½" of the front and back to the leg pieces. Drill a 1½"-diameter hole under the center of the head into the body cavity. Drill ½"-wide holes ⅛" deep with a spade bit for eyes. Glue a 1½"-diameter tapered plug to the back of the head. File and sand round and smooth. Apply finish as desired.

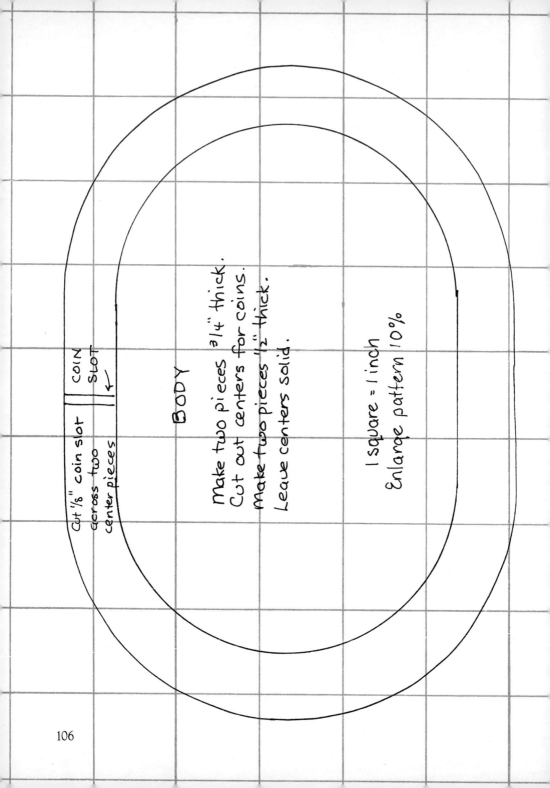

Cut 1/8" coin slot across two center pieces

COIN SLOT

BODY

Make two pieces 3/4" thick.
Cut out centers for coins.
Make two pieces 1/2" thick.
Leave centers solid.

1 square = 1 inch
Enlarge pattern 10%

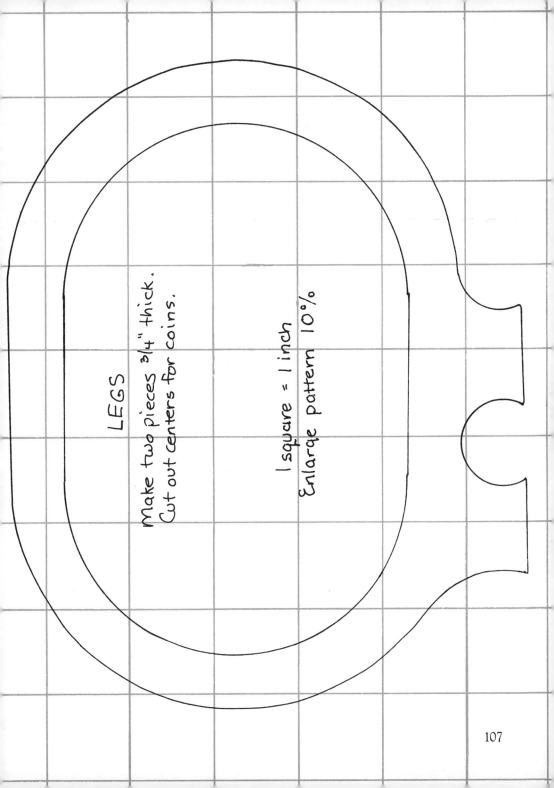

LEGS

Make two pieces 3/4" thick.
Cut out centers for coins.

1 square = 1 inch
Enlarge pattern 10%

107

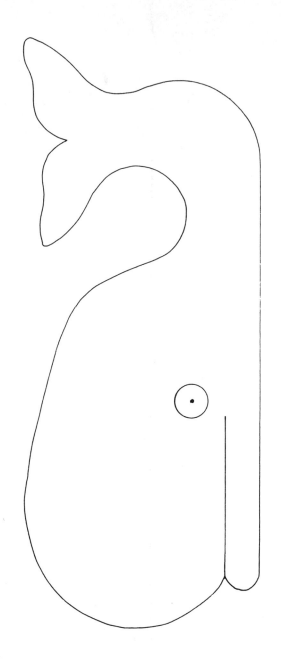

WHALE

Lay out all parts on ¾″-thick wood. Note grain direction on parts "A" and "B". Cut the parts out to shape. Be careful to make a clean, thin cut through "A", cutting the tail off. These parts must fit back together as the tail tilts for access to the money. With the parts cut out, glue the front half of part "A" between the two "B" parts. With a damp rag, remove all glue that squeezes out where the tail will be inserted.

When the glue has set, fit the tail piece into the slot. Be sure the tail is in the correct position and then carefully drill a ¼″-wide hole through all three pieces. Tap a ¼″ × 2¼″ dowel into the hole with a hammer. When the dowel is about halfway in try to move the tail down. If the tail binds, remove the dowel and file or sand the parts where they touch. When the parts move freely, tap the dowel all the way in flush with the surface. Glue the "C" parts to the sides of "B". Cut the mouth slot by sawing across all five pieces. Starting behind the eyes, saw the sides at an angle into the tail. Drill the eyes ⅛″ deep with a ½″-spade bit. File and sand the edges round and smooth.

The whale can be made with a spout if desired. Cut the spout out of ¾″ wood, file the edges round, taper the end to ⁵⁄₁₆″ round. Stain the spout blue. Drill a ⁵⁄₁₆″ hole in the top of the whale and insert the spout. Finish the whale as desired.

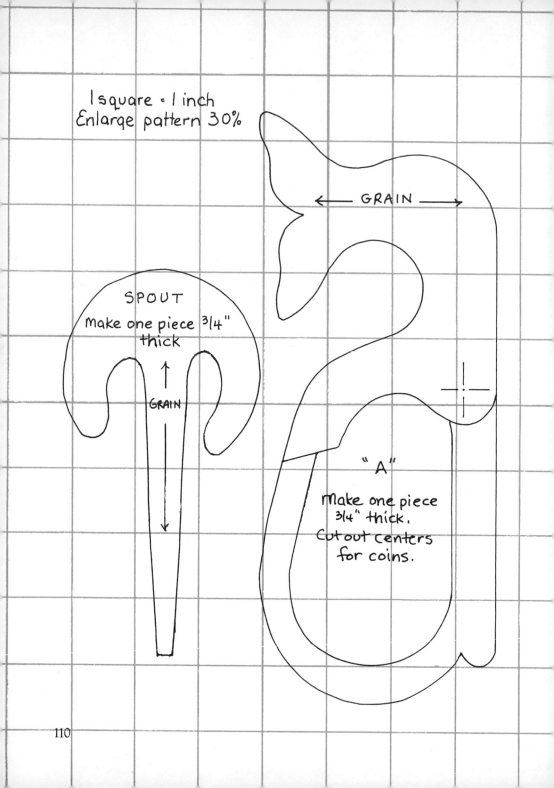

1 square = 1 inch
Enlarge pattern 30%

← GRAIN →

SPOUT
Make one piece 3/4"
thick

↑ GRAIN ↓

"A"
Make one piece
3/4" thick.
Cut out centers
for coins.

110

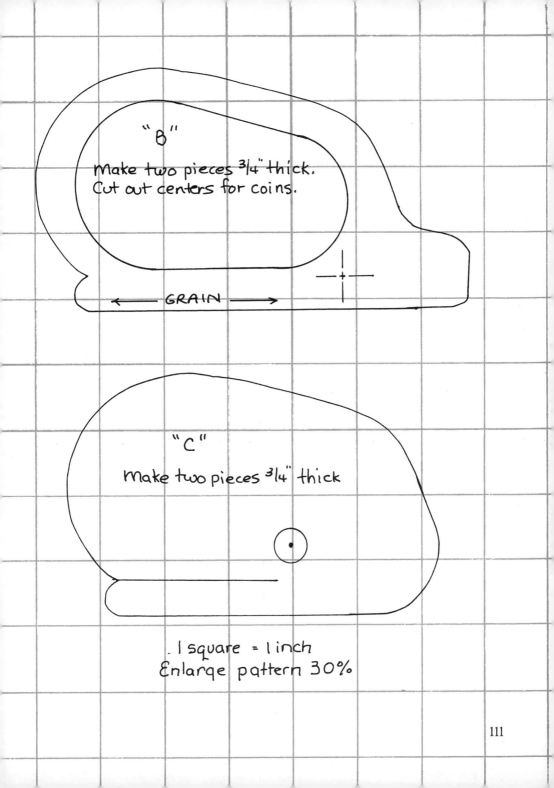

"B"

Make two pieces ¾" thick.
Cut out centers for coins.

← GRAIN →

"C"

Make two pieces ¾" thick

1 square = 1 inch
Enlarge pattern 30%

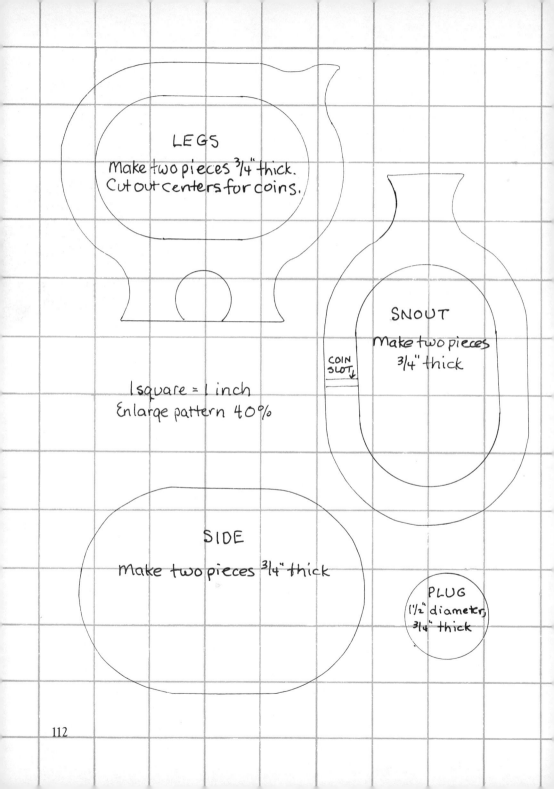

LEGS

Make two pieces ¾" thick.
Cut out centers for coins.

SNOUT

Make two pieces
¾" thick

COIN
SLOT↓

1 square = 1 inch
Enlarge pattern 40%

SIDE

Make two pieces ¾" thick

PLUG
1½" diameter,
¾" thick

112

THE PIGGY BANK

Lay out the leg and nose parts on ¾″-thick wood. The sides are ½″ thick. Cut the parts to shape. The inside can be drilled out with the 2½″ hole saw making two cuts in each piece. Glue the two nose (center) pieces together and when dry cut a ⅛″ coin slot across the top into the center. Glue the leg and side pieces to the nose pieces. Drill the eyes with a ½″ spade bit. Drill the nose holes with just the point of the spade bit or with a ³⁄₁₆″ twist drill. Drill a 1½″-diameter hole between the legs into the center cavity. Fit a 1½″-diameter, ¾″-thick tapered plug into this hole for coin removal. Rasp, file, and sand the pig round and smooth. The pig needs a lot of filing and sanding to look good. Apply finish as desired.

The pig can also be made with a removable nose instead of a bottom plug. Use the same patterns but cut the nose off and drill a 1½″-diameter hole into the cavity. Glue two ¾″-thick × 1½″-diameter plugs together to make a cylinder 1½″ diameter × 1½″ long. Sand a taper on one end to fit tightly into the hole.

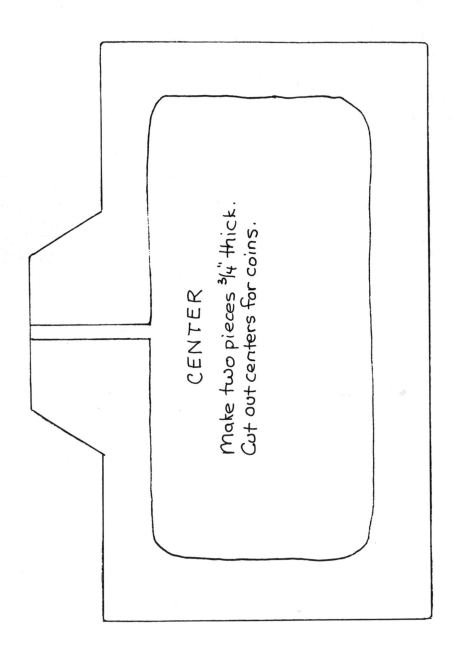

CENTER

Make two pieces ³/₄" thick.
Cut out centers for coins.

114

CAMERA

Lay out the camera body on the wood, two pieces ¾" × 4¼" × 6" and two pieces ½" × 4¼" × 6". Cut the pieces to size. Glue the two ¾" pieces together. When dry, cut out the center starting with the ⅛"-wide coin slot. Glue the ½"-thick front and back to the body. You will now have a block 2½" × 4¼" × 6". Cut across the top and down to form the viewfinder. File and sand the front of the viewfinder on an angle to the coin slot. Drill a ½"-wide hole ⅛" deep into the back of the viewfinder to simulate an eyepiece. Drill ¼" holes for the shutter release, and drill holes for dowels for knobs. Drill a 1½"-diameter hole through the front into the cavity to receive the lens and give access to the money.

Lay out the lens parts and knobs. Cut the parts to shape. Cut the inside of the lens shade, and sand it. Then glue it to the lens, and cut, file, and sand the outside. Glue the lens-back and plug to the lens and fit the plug into the hole in the body. Insert dowels in the holes and knobs onto the dowels. Rasp and file the bank to shape, cutting the corners off at 45°. Finish as desired.

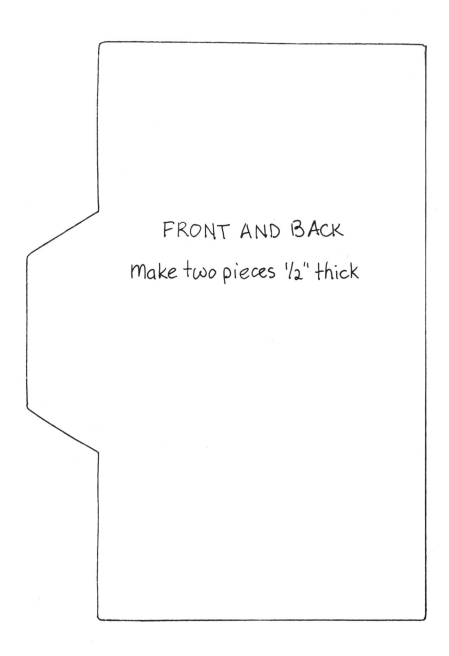

FRONT AND BACK

Make two pieces ½" thick

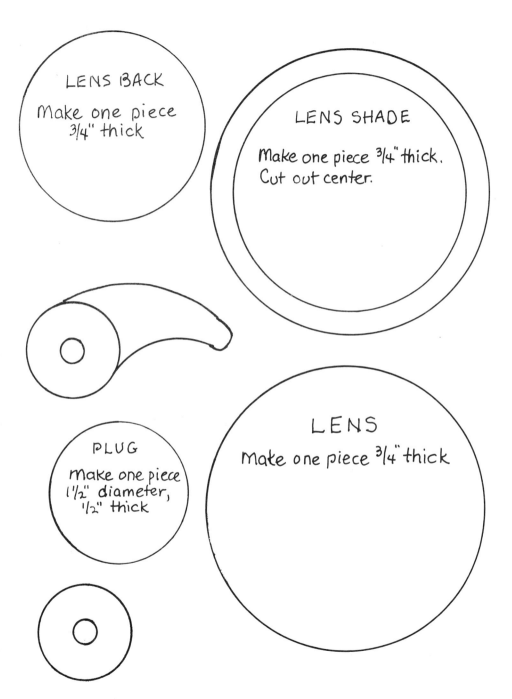

LENS BACK

Make one piece
3/4" thick

LENS SHADE

Make one piece 3/4" thick.
Cut out center.

PLUG

make one piece
1 1/2" diameter,
1/2" thick

LENS

Make one piece 3/4" thick

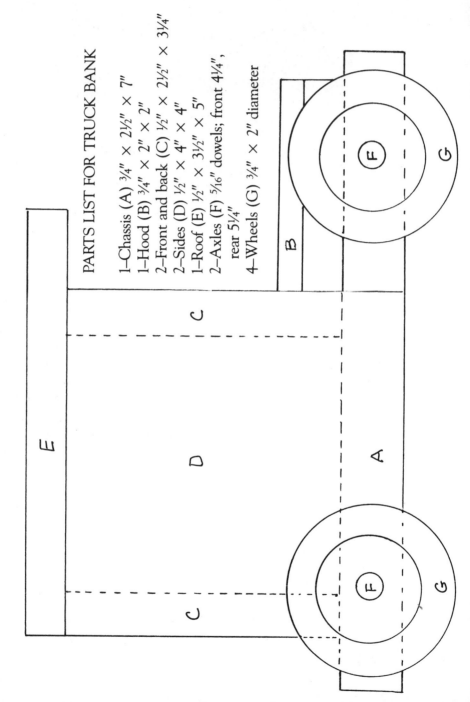

PARTS LIST FOR TRUCK BANK

1–Chassis (A) ¾" × 2½" × 7"
1–Hood (B) ¾" × 2" × 2"
2–Front and back (C) ½" × 2½" × 3¼"
2–Sides (D) ½" × 4" × 4"
1–Roof (E) ½" × 3½" × 5"
2–Axles (F) 5⁄16" dowels; front 4¼", rear 5¼"
4–Wheels (G) ¾" × 2" diameter

TRUCK

All the parts of the truck are squares or rectangles except the wheels and axles. The edges must be square to the face of each piece. This is quite difficult with hand tools, but if you have access to a table saw the parts can be cut straight and square in a few minutes. The chassis is ¾″ × 2½″ × 7″. Drill a ⅜″-wide hole 2″ from the front, in the center of the ¾″ edge. This hole goes clear through the chassis. The hood is ¾″ × 2″ × 2″. Drill two ½″-wide holes in front and glue ¼″ dowels for headlights. (Note: This can also be done with a plug cutter in a ¼″ electric drill in one operation.) Make the front and back ½″ × 2½″ × 3¼″. Nail the front to the back of the hood. Be sure they are lined up correctly. Drill a ¼″-diameter hole through the ½″ front into the hood about ½″ deep. Pull the front off the hood and remove the nails. Glue a ¼″ dowel 1″ long into the hole in the hood. Make the two sides ½″ × 4″ × 4″ and the roof ½″ × 3½″ × 5″. Cut a ⅛″ × 1½″ coin slot in the roof. Nail and glue the sides to the front and back. Nail the roof on top with the front sticking out over the hood. Fit the chassis between the sides and drill a ⅜″-wide hole 1¼″ from the back through the sides and the chassis.

Make the wheels ¾″ × 2″ diameter by drilling with a hole saw. Drill out the centers of the wheels with a ⁵⁄₁₆″ drill to accept the ⁵⁄₁₆″ dowels as axles. The front axle is 4¼″ long and the rear axle is 5¼″ long. Enlarge the hole in the front to fit easily on the dowel in the hood. With the body in place on the chassis and the rear axle inserted, glue the hood in place on the front of the chassis. To get the money out, remove one rear wheel, sliding the axle out and pulling the body back off the dowel in the hood. The wheels are pressed onto the axles. (If the fit is too tight tap lightly with a hammer.) Do not sand the axles. They will loosen a bit with use. Sand until smooth, and finish as desired.

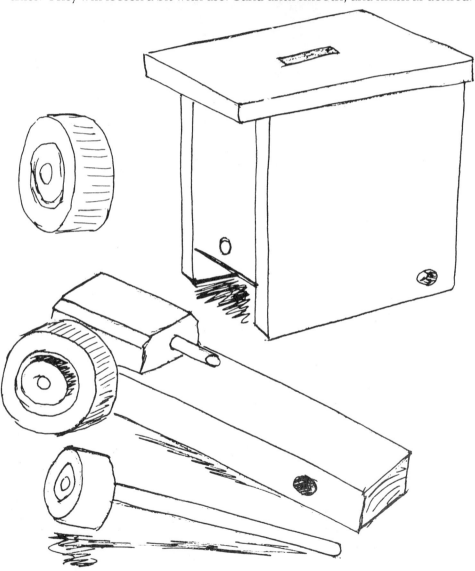

HIPPO

Lay out the parts on ¾"-thick wood and cut to shape. Drill eyes ⅛" deep with a ½" spade bit. Drill ⁵⁄₁₆" holes ¼" deep for teeth. Glue the two center pieces together and cut a ⅛"-wide coin slot across the top into the center. I put the coin slot between the eyes, but it can go anywhere on top. Glue the sides to this center section. Drill a 1½"-diameter hole into the body cavity under one of the hind legs. Make a tapered plug to fit tightly into this hole. Glue the plug to the back of the hind leg. Glue the other three legs to the body. Glue and tap the teeth into the holes. File and sand all edges round and smooth. Finish as desired.

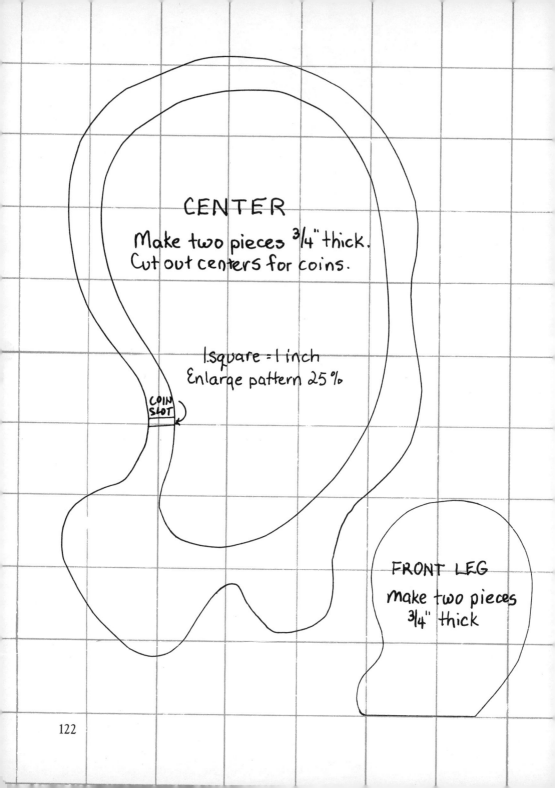

CENTER

Make two pieces ¾" thick.
Cut out centers for coins.

1 square = 1 inch
Enlarge pattern 25%

COIN
SLOT

FRONT LEG

make two pieces
¾" thick

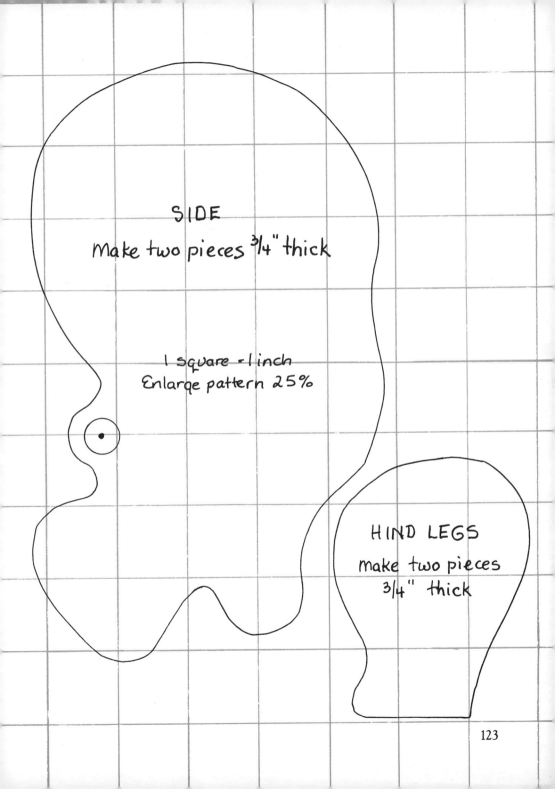

SIDE

Make two pieces ¾" thick

1 square = 1 inch
Enlarge pattern 25%

HIND LEGS

make two pieces
¾" thick

123

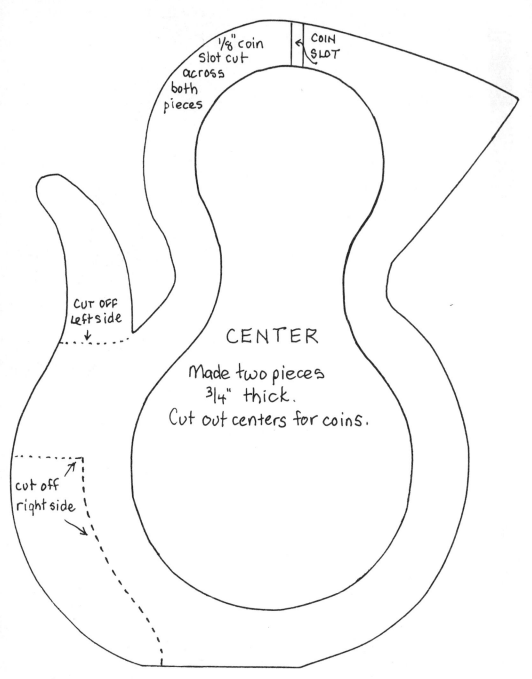

1/8" coin Slot cut across both pieces

COIN SLOT

CUT OFF Left side

CENTER

Made two pieces 3/4" thick.
Cut out centers for coins.

cut off right side

MOUSE

Lay out the parts on the wood. The two center parts and the legs are ¾" thick. The rest of the parts are ½" thick. Cut the parts to shape. The center pieces are made into left and right sides by cutting the tail on the dotted line for each side. These pieces are glued together and the tail is shaped to curve in an "s" shape. Cut a ⅛"-wide coin slot across the top of these two pieces (between the ears). Glue the body sides and head sides to the two center pieces. Drill a 1⅜"-diameter hole though one side of the head under the ear. Rasp and file the mouse to shape. The nose is cone-shaped. Some of the waste wood can be sawed off the nose to save time and work. Glue the arms, legs, and ear without the hole to the body. Glue a 1⅜"-diameter tapered plug to the back of the other ear to fit the hole. Sand until smooth and finish as desired.

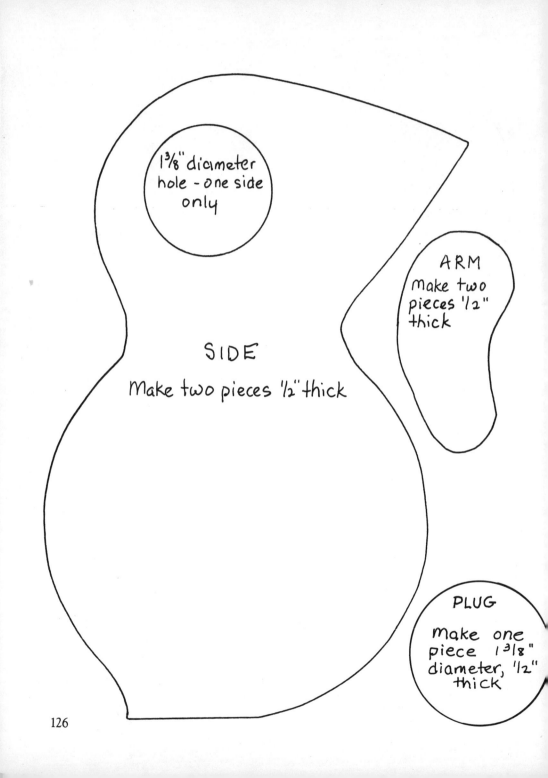

1³⁄₈" diameter hole - one side only

ARM
make two pieces ¹⁄₂" thick

SIDE

Make two pieces ¹⁄₂" thick

PLUG

make one piece 1³⁄₈" diameter, ¹⁄₂" thick

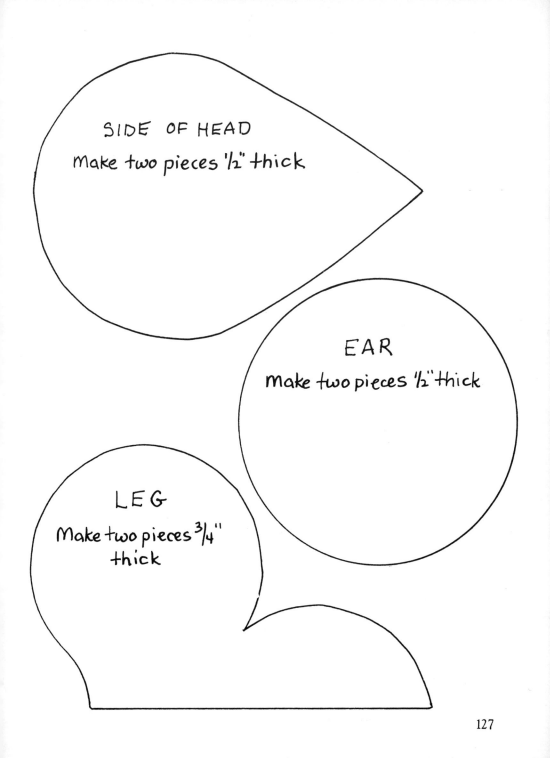

SIDE OF HEAD
Make two pieces ½" thick

EAR
Make two pieces ½" thick

LEG
Make two pieces ¾" thick

INDEX